Giving Candy to Strangers

Growing Your Business
Can be as Fun & Easy as...

Giving
Candy to
Strangers

*Tips for Creating Abundance
through Heart-Centered Sales*

Stan Holden

Growing Your Business Can be as Fun & Easy as...Giving Candy To Strangers
Tips for Creating Abundance Through Heart-Centered Sales
Copyright ©2015 by Stan Holden
Cover design by Stan Holden. Illustrations by D.C. Roberts.
Back cover photo by Scott Tokar
All rights reserved.

Published by Next Century Publishing
Las Vegas, Nevada
www.NextCenturyPublishing.com

ISBN: 9781629038575
Library of Congress Control Number: 2015940873

Printed in the United States of America

CONTENTS

Foreword...13

Introduction..15

PART 1: Creating Connections Without an Agenda 19

#1   Play in the Sandbox... 23

#2   Name Names.. 27

#3   Always Be Opening... 30

#4   Make an Old Friend.. 32

#5   Get Your Ducks in a Flow 34

#6   Know Your "Why" 37

#7   Expect Failure 40

#8   Play By the Two Rules... 43

PART 2: Nurturing Your Existing Relationships 47

#9   Be Friendfull 49

#10   Track Your Tribe... 52

#11   Play Rolodex Roulette... 54

#12   Make Contagious Connections 56

#13   Count Your Bacon 58

#14   Don't Let Your Friends Grow Up to be Strangers....... 61

PART 3: Overcoming Common Obstacles to Connection 65

#15   Forget About What Others Think 67

#16   Unmask Yourself 68

#17   Invite People to Laugh at You............................. 71

#18   Sell Your Story.. 72

#19   Rehearse Your Story 76

#20   Write Your Own Rejection Letter 78

#21   Exude Empathy 83

#22   Do What's Right When No One Is Looking 85

PART 4: Understanding Strangers................................ 89

#23   Don't Judge a Cook by His Brother................... 91

#24   Be Unassuming 96

#25   Look, Learn, and Listen 98

#26   When in Rome, Talk to Strangers 102

#27   Practice the Care and Feeding of Celebrities........ 104

#28   Don't Put People on Pedestals...................... 107

#29   Be Nice to the Gatekeepers 110

#30   Squeak Your Wheel 113

PART 5: Using Humor to Create Connection 117

#31   Get In Your Discomfort Zone 120

#32   Break the Nice 124

#33   Go Full Foolocity 129

#34   Remember, Timing Is Everything................. 132

#35   Go Fishing 134

#36   Play Up Your Title...................................... 136

PART 6: Cold Calling and Other Atrocities 139

#37   Do Mix Pleasure with Business 143

#38   If You're Trying to Sell, Say So...................... 145

#39   Never Write Off a Wrong Number................ 149

#40   Kiss More Toads... 151

#41   Go People Watching 154

#42   Do Your Homework 159

PART 7: Building Relationships Through Social Media 163

#43   Give Virtual Candy 166

#44   Facebook It 169

#45   Link in to LinkedIn 172

#46   Tweet Them Right 175

PART 8: Leveraging Your Relationships 179

#47   Become a Matchmaker................................. 181

#48   Create Win-Wins 185

#49   Practice Random Acts of Sales...................... 187

#50   Be an Opportunity Maker............................ 190

#51   Make Someone's Day 193

#52   Make a New Friend..................................... 195

Thank You... 200

Endnotes... 204

For Sara, William, Renée, Jack, and Bella

We sometimes encounter people, even perfect strangers, who begin to interest us at first sight, somehow suddenly, all at once, before a word has been spoken.
Fyodor Dostoevsky

Life is about relationship, not acquisition.
Rick Warren

FOREWORD

by Kevin Sorbo

As an actor, I am an artist in the "business" of people—the business of motivating, inspiring, and eliciting feelings in them, through which many unilateral relationships are forged with perfect strangers. From my television show *Hercules: The Legendary Journeys,* known as the most popular show on earth when it aired, those relationships grew into the millions. As my career progressed, many more have been created beyond that.

My fans come to know me through my work, but to reciprocate those relationships is, of course, impossible. An actor's persona and story on-screen only goes in one direction, but the "business" that happens off screen is a story of a different sort.

I met Stan a few years ago at a pre–Academy Awards party. He was representing one of the many companies that were promoting products through this event. I had passed by his booth unintentionally, not really noticing that I had done so. Stan, however, did notice and eventually found me in the lobby and struck up a short conversation. He handed me his card and I went on my way. We never spoke about business.

Stan's business card did indeed resurface a couple of weeks later as I was sending out invites to a celebrity golf tournament that I was hosting. I sent him an e-mail, thinking that his company might be interested in sponsorship. After several back-and-forth e-mails, I decided to pick up the phone and just give him a call. A much lengthier conversation than our first transpired, during which he mentioned that he wanted to give me a product that he was promoting; he felt it could dramatically change my life. (Later, I found out that Stan had no idea that I had suffered three strokes while filming the final season of "Hercules"; his product helped me in this area.) This was the start of a uniquely formed friendship.

I believe that everything happens for a reason. Meeting Stan that night was proof to me of that belief. In a city and profession where honesty is at a premium and everyone seems to be working you for something, Stan's authentic energy, honesty, and humor were very refreshing. Since then, we have collaborated on a number of different projects. No longer are we strangers, but good friends. His enthusiasm for life, which I have come to know and appreciate, is at the heart of Giving Candy to Strangers.

What strikes me is that when doing business with Stan, you don't notice the business. "Have fun," Stan always says when we sign off from a call—and that is the enduring message of this book: Do business with the joy of a kid.

The pleasure of our day-to-day experiences and the experiences we leave with others is so much more important than money, but with this attitude, money will follow. *Giving Candy to Strangers* is a must read for anyone looking to create and enhance their professional and personal relationships in a new and refreshing way.

Kevin Sorbo, *actor, producer, entrepreneur*

INTRODUCTION

"How many of you were introduced to this company by a total stranger?"

The speaker, my good friend and mentor K. Ross, looked around the packed hotel ballroom, where more than 2,500 people were gathered to learn about sales and recruiting. A couple dozen hands went up, and Ross encouraged them to stand. With an affirming nod, he explained to his audience, "They call what we do *relationship marketing* for a reason." For him, those few people standing in such a crowded room illustrated his point—the way to grow a sales network is through existing relationships. For me, however, they illustrated something different. You see, of those two dozen people who raised their hands, more than half of them had been introduced to the company by me. A total stranger.

As I looked out over the sea of heads, I realized that I am an exception to one of the time-tested rules of my industry. I introduce strangers to my business all the time, so I must be doing something right, even if it's a little unorthodox, because I've built a network of hundreds of thousands of people worldwide.

Maybe I didn't listen to my parents when they told me—as I am sure yours did too—never to talk to strangers. In my adult years, it did not come naturally to me, but now it's one of my favorite things to do. And as for that other common piece of childhood advice, I've turned it on its head: I make a habit of *giving* candy to strangers on a regular basis.

"Giving candy to strangers" is a metaphor for stepping out of your comfort zone and creating new relationships in a spirit of generosity and openness, without trying to engineer any particular kind of outcome. It's about making connections in a creative and fun way. What's the candy? Well, it can be simply your time and attention. Or it might be a fun little gift in place of a business card (I'll talk more about this in #33). Sometimes, you won't know what the candy is until you start the conversation and find out how you can help. The point is that you come to each new connection with an attitude of "what can I give?" rather than "what can I get?" You "pay it forward" with each hand you shake and smile you share.

I wasn't always a salesman. As a matter of fact I once loathed the entire notion. I have, however, always been a connector. My training and talents lie in the field of art and design, and for many years I ran a successful design studio. I lived and breathed by word-of-mouth advertising, and thanks to the connections I built, I had the pleasure of working with many large companies like Disney, Apple, Isuzu, and Warner Brothers. Eventually, however, the economic downturn forced me to look elsewhere so I turned sales to help provide for my family. I began to apply the lessons I had learned from my creative career to my new profession, and was surprised to discover how many of them held true, particularly when it came to building relationships.

Business books written by artists are a rarity. And for a good reason; most artists are not good business people. Business did not come naturally to me either, but I have always brought a spirit of creativity to my profession, and because of that my design studio flourished and became quite successful. Later, as I applied that same strategy to my sales career, it too flourished and far exceeded my expectations!

When I started down the path of sales, I was insecure about my lack of experience. But I soon realized that my lack of experience was really a blessing and, in fact, my greatest strength. It allowed me to do things creatively and diverge from the norm. And, although it might seem like a world of difference between being an artist and being a salesman, the two were less far apart than I might have expected. I like to say that I went from being a creative professional to a professional creative. And the bridge between the two was my unorthodox approach to relationship building.

There are many books out there that will teach you how to build business relationships step-by-step. This is not one of them. Here you will learn to do it without systems, rules, limitations, or barriers. Think of this book not as a recipe, but rather as a menu of creative ideas and ingredients that you can sample, adapt, or combine as you like. And most importantly, have fun while you use it (hence, my irreverent humor throughout!). It's not a "how-to-do" guide; it's a "how-to-be" guide. If you're having fun and meeting strangers in a spirit of generosity, curiosity, and possibility, you'll find that before you know it you'll have new friends, new colleagues, and yes, new sales!

As you read this book, I encourage you to put the ideas and suggestions into practice as soon as you set it aside and step out your front door. Don't wait until you've reached the end and become an expert. Start practicing as you read the very first chapter. You can read about swimming all you would like, but in order to actually swim you have to jump into the pool! In each section, I'll be offering suggestions, exercises, and experiments you can try wherever you are. I hope this book will inspire and motivate you to get out there and give some candy to strangers!

Have Fun!

Stan

PART 1

Building Relationships Without an Agenda

In the early nineteenth century, the French bohemians coined a popular phrase, "l'art pour l'art," which is commonly translated into English as "art for art's sake." They used this slogan in defiance of those who claimed that art should have a purpose, such as conveying some moral lesson. Art is valuable for itself, they retaliated. It does not need to carry a message to justify its existence.

As a professional graphic designer with bills to pay, I can't claim to have had the luxury of being an "art for art's sake" kind of artist during my commercial career, although I certainly was familiar with the axiom during my college days. I had created such masterpieces as "The Three Maps of Combustion," a triptych made by the burning of carpet with a blowtorch and other incendiaries—yes, I almost left this earth too early for my art. However, the spirit of that old slogan is something I've always appreciated, and I've found it to be very applicable when it comes to the art of building relationships.

There are many experts out there who will teach you about how to build business relationships for the sake of achieving specific outcomes—making sales, getting referrals, establishing influence, and so on. They will offer you step-by-step formulas and detailed strategies for making your connections count. They will show you how to measure the effectiveness of your communication skills and improve your success rates.

Here's the problem I see with that approach: People are not a commodity. Too many salespeople treat their "prospects" as just a few more notches on their gun belts, and this is a big part of what gives sales a bad rap. They are focused on the end result, the outcome—the close. What if you approached "sales" from a people-focused, heart-centered standpoint? What if you created relationships for no other reason than to help others and make new friends?

I've always been fond of wordplay and double entendres, and while writing about the idea of "art for art's sake" as it applies to building relationships, it occurred to me that "Art" is also a name. Do I have a relationship with anyone named Art? *I wondered. I scanned my mental Rolodex (yes, I'm old enough that I have one of those), but no one came to mind.* Well, I'm writing a book about connecting with strangers, *I thought,* so why not put it into practice. *As a personal challenge, I set out to create a relationship with a stranger named Art, for no other reason than the fact that his name is Art, and see where it would lead me.* No matter what the outcome, *I decided,* I'll share the story in the book. *Therefore, I'm creating a story (art) for the sake of the book (art for art's sake).*

I searched the Internet for a stranger named Art and stumbled across the LinkedIn page of a gentleman named Art Flater. He is the president and owner of Central 3D Systems, a 3D printer reseller. I was attracted to his page because of his very funny profile and the fact that he is in sales himself, so I figured he might be open to a totally cold call from a stranger with a quirky anti-agenda. So I picked up the phone and dialed Art.

I introduced myself and explained why I was calling. Art was intrigued, and we ended up chatting for almost an hour. I now have a new friend who plans on "me buying him" a drink when he next visits California. He is now also aware of my talents and service, so perhaps he'll become a client. Either way, it was a great connection, and I'm not concerned about the results.

I know what you are thinking: How can it not be about the results when it comes to business? I've got a family to feed! I can't afford to play around making random friends and cold-calling strangers I found on the Internet just to chat. I've got sales quotas to meet and bills to pay. *I understand how you feel. I too have to deal with the day-to-day demands of making a living, and I'm not saying the bottom line is unimportant. What I'm saying is that if you let go of this burden while you are creating relationships, you will find that the health of your bottom line will improve!*

There are times when an agenda is necessary, such as in cold-calling (see Part 6). But in my opinion, when done correctly, the heart and soul of great, long-term sales is creating ongoing relationships for their own sake. It's about building connections that can evolve, mature, grow in trust, and reciprocate. When you create relationships without immediately trying to engineer a specific outcome, you invest in the future growth of your business by expanding your greatest asset—your circle of connections. You may not be able to immediately calculate the results of your efforts or put them in a balance sheet, but trust me, over time you will see the impact in measurable terms. The greatest salespeople are those who love people—who enjoy meeting and getting to know strangers from all walks of life. And if you don't feel like you're one of those yet, the good news is that it can be learned! Let's get started...

FUN FACT

Ironically, the phrase "art for art's sake" is sometimes used commercially. The movie studio Metro-Goldwyn-Mayer uses a Latin version of the phrase, *ars gratia artis*, as a motto—you can see it in the circle around the roaring head of Leo the Lion in their logo. I wonder if the well-compensated studio executives realize what the message in their motto means?

*One of the most obvious facts about grown-ups, to a child,
is that they have forgotten what it is like to be a child.*
Randall Jarrell

#1

Play in the Sandbox

*There are no strangers here; only
friends we haven't yet met.*
William Butler Yeats

When my kids were young, my wife and I would often take them to the park to burn off their pent-up energy and "get their yahoos out." In reality, we needed it more than they did! Before the minivan door had closed behind them, they would tear off to the playset with a rooster tail of wood chips, grass, and sand at their heels and scatter among the other kids—talking, playing, and relating as though they had known them for years.

Were our kids unique that way? No, all kids are like that. Unhindered by inhibitions, they are creative and curious, playful and free. They look at the world with childlike wonder, free from preconceived notions about others. Of course, not all others are to be trusted, and that's why we have to teach our children to be careful. But most of us could stand to learn a thing or two from watching children relate to strangers in the sandbox and benefit by recapturing some of that unguarded innocence and openness— while shedding a few of our fears, suspicions, and inhibitions—as we make new friends.

If you learn anything from this book, I would like it to be that. My aim is not to teach you something you do not already know, but to encourage you to dump your proverbial toy chest of experience and ideas on the ground, mix them up with others, and playfully look at the world in a different light.

I encourage you to meet strangers on the street like you used to meet kids at the playground.

Just because it's something that once came naturally to you doesn't mean it will be easy now. The great artist Picasso is believed to have said, "It took me four years to paint like Raphael, but a lifetime to paint like a child." In order to learn to relate like a child, you may need to overcome some deep-seated habits and inhibitions. You may have to let go of much of what you've been taught about how to be a successful salesperson, and even put aside your "business sense" for a while.

As adults, we often adhere to preconceived notions of how our worlds should be. This is great when it comes to keeping control of our little worlds but terrible when it comes to creating something new and different. Sometimes too much experience can encumber our creativity and spontaneity. I once heard someone say, "You're going to make more money than you are smart enough to make." I'm not sure if that was a compliment or not, but it cuts right to core of what I'm getting at: we don't know what we don't know. And sometimes that can be a good thing!

Several notable people have been accredited with saying, "The only thing that interferes with my learning is my education." Of course, I'm not saying that knowledge and experience is bad. However, sometimes we get tripped up by how we *think* we should be going about our "business" based on what experience or education tells us. We limit ourselves to what we know and don't give ourselves the freedom to try creative or unusual approaches. So I'm encouraging you to set aside whatever assumptions you have—even those you consider tried and tested truths—at least for the time it takes you to read this book and experiment with putting my ideas into practice.

Speaking of putting things into practice, even though we are only a few pages into this book, I want you to do that right now. When you finish reading this section, put down the book (in a place that you will remember because I, of course, want you to keep reading it), go out into the street, and find a public place where people are gathered. This will be your sandbox. Maybe it's your local park, or the bus stop down the block, or the corner store. You're going to give some candy to strangers.

Wait a minute, you may be thinking. *I don't have anything to give to people.* That is where you are wrong. One of the simplest and most powerful things you can give someone is your openness and warmth. A big, trusting smile is a beautiful gift! And that's all you need for this particular exercise. We will get into more elaborate forms of candy-giving later.

So here's what you're going to do. Imagine you're six years old, and the world is your sandbox. Try to put aside your grown-up inhibitions and suspicions, and get yourself into the open, trusting, curious mind-set of a child. Can you feel it? If it helps, wear flip flops, a bright-colored t-shirt, or a silly hat, or watch a funny or inspiring movie beforehand. Try writing a letter to your inner child; you never know what will come out—anything that helps you feel in tune *with* your inner child and less like a stuffy adult. Once you're in touch with that feeling, it's time to go out and play!

When you get to a public place, all I want you to do is to look at each person and imagine that person is already your friend or a family member. The woman pushing her kids in a stroller—imagine she's someone you went to school with. The guy hailing a cab and talking on his cell phone—think of him as a cousin you used to climb trees with. Even the homeless guy asleep on the park bench—perhaps he's someone you used to work with, who's fallen on hard times. Do this for each person you encounter.

As you imagine each person as a friend, notice what happens to your face. You should feel your defenses relaxing, your brows unfurrowing, and the corners of your mouth starting to lift. Let yourself break into a big, warm smile as you look at all of these friends.

That's all. You don't need to engage with anyone, unless they initiate a conversation. If they smile back and strike up a conversation, that's great— see where it takes you. But for the purposes of this exercise, don't try to make that happen. Just give them the kind of smile you would give to an old friend, and don't look for anything in return.

Try it, and notice how you feel after you've been doing this for half an hour. You may be surprised at how good it feels to start treating strangers like friends.

If you want to try an advanced version of this exercise, go to a place that's particularly crowded, busy, and intense—a train station at rush hour, a big city street in the middle of the day, a grocery store on the day before Thanksgiving. Get right in the middle of the crowd. If you have errands to run or places to get to yourself, even better.

First, notice how you feel. It's likely to be overwhelming—the crush of people, the heightened stress of too many bodies in a small place, the irritation of everyone trying to get to where they're going, all at once. Don't be too hard on yourself if you're not feeling too friendly toward all these strangers who are getting in your way—that's a common response.

If you are a seasoned conventional salesperson, at this point you may be thinking that this is too soft or touchy-feely. But hang in there—that's the whole point. I am trying to get you into a different mind-set.

As Australian writer Samuel Leighton-Dore observes in a wonderful article for the online magazine *Thought Catalog*, "It's easy to lose sight of the beauty in strangers...We see them as obstacles, shadows ahead of us—always walking just that much slower than we'd like, selfishly stepping into ticket queues the moment before we do. Don't they know we're running late? Don't they know we have somewhere to be? Strangers inconvenience our schedules; they're the blurred, unpaid extras to our blockbuster, personal narratives—and we don't have the time, we don't have the patience."

In the midst of a moment like that, try the exercise above. Forget about your schedule and your story and instead imagine theirs. See each of them as a close friend. As Leighton-Dore reflects, doing this "makes me realize that the crowd doesn't have to be an ocean in which to drown—but a sea in which to swim. It breaks down the walls—you know, the ones we all put up as we leave the house each morning."[1]

Pick the most challenging moment in the busiest place you can find, and try this. Do it when you're in a hurry and everyone else is moving slowly. Do it when you're late for work and there's a line of thirty people ahead of you trying to get on an already-full bus. Do it when all you want to do is pay for your groceries and get home after a long day at work, and the person in front of you at the checkout is digging around in her purse for a wad of coupons. Do it at those moments when you're feeling like the most important person in the world and everyone else just seems like an obstacle (or whatever word you would normally use).

Embrace interruptions and you will notice that your anxiety level in busy situations will dissipate. Watch how your frustrations melt away when you start to feel like you're surrounded by friends you just haven't met yet.

#2

Name Names

*The beginning of wisdom is to call
things by their right names.*
Chinese Proverb

The quickest way to make a stranger feel like a friend is to remember his or her name. But that's easier said than done. One of the reasons that the classic comedy routine "Who's On First?" by Abbot and Costello was so popular (some say it is the most famous comedy sketch of all time) is because we can all relate to how hard it can be to keep track of people's names.

I'm sure you've had one of these awkward moments. You're at a party, or a conference or some other social event, and you've made a new acquaintance. She's just introduced herself as Sandra, and you're having a great conversation, when one of your colleagues approaches. "Hey Jim!" you say. And then there's a silence. Your new acquaintance is waiting for you to introduce her to your colleague, but you've already forgotten her name! Or perhaps you have run into an acquaintance at the market who says hello, and you stare back blankly at him, before mumbling, "Ah, hey—you—ah, how are you doing?"

If you are one of those people who finds it difficult to remember names, fear not, you're not alone—many people report the same affliction. I know that it's something I have struggled with. I refer to it as "Whosit's" disease. Research has found that it's harder to remember people's names than it is to remember their jobs, hobbies, or hometowns.[2] And according to Gary Small, M.D., in *Psychology Today*, this issue just worsens with age, as nearly

85 percent of middle-aged and older adults forget names.[3] Why is that? Because it's easier to attach a visual reminder to a job or a hobby than it is to a nondescript name. And the human memory is very visually oriented.

Don't let Whosit's disease get you! Remembering names is an important skill. Have you ever met someone important, successful, or famous and been surprised when he or she addresses you by name, or remembers personal details you thought he or she would never have even paid attention to? That's because successful people know the power of a name.

A friend of mine, Emma, who is a writer, told me a story about how she recently attended a writer's conference. The conference had been running for more than a decade, and it had been founded by a guy who was a very successful literary agent. There were about three hundred people at the event, all aspiring authors who were there to network with the agents and publishers who could hopefully offer them a book deal. On the first night, everyone gathered in the hotel ballroom for a cocktail party. Emma walked in, and the first person she saw was the founder of the conference. Amazingly, no one else was waiting to talk to him, so she took a deep breath, walked up, and introduced herself. Within the space of a few minutes, he mentioned two people he thought she should connect with, and a half hour later, he sought her out among the crowd, bringing one of them with him, and introduced her by name. She was surprised and grateful he took the time. The next day, he was giving a keynote, and Emma raised her hand during the Q&A. He looked across the room and saw her, and without missing a beat, asked, "Emma, did you have a question?"

Emma was shocked that the most important guy in the room remembered the name of a stranger he'd met for only a couple of minutes during a party at which he probably had fifty such interactions with authors eager to get published. I wasn't surprised at all. It's no accident that the most successful guy there had exceptional relationship skills. They are probably a big part of what got him to where he is.

Keith Ferrazzi, business relationships expert and author of *Never Eat Alone*, writes: "Remembering a name tells someone that they made a memorable impression, and that you cared enough to remember them."[4] And his number one tip for remembering names is: "Make a choice to care. . . . If you make a conscious decision that you are going to remember names, because you care about the people you meet, you will immediately become much better at doing it!" Keith is right. One of the primary reasons we forget each other so easily is that we don't really care. We aren't fully paying attention in the first place. If you are worrying about yourself, or what you can get out of a relationship, or what you're going to say, you're not really listening. So really, this is another way of giving candy to strangers: give them your full, undivided attention when they introduce themselves.

In addition to this all-important shift of attention, here are a couple of tricks you can use to improve your memory.

The simplest tool is repetition. It's easier to remember something when you say it than it is when you simply hear it. If you meet a woman and she tells you her name is Tiffany (there's always a Tiffany), say it right back to her: "Nice to meet you, Tiffany." Or if a guy tells you his name is Jack, use his name when you're asking him a question: "Where do you live, Jack?"

Another tool you can use is to practice associating a person's name with something that will help you remember, preferably a visual image. We remember better in images than we do in words. So if you meet a guy named Bryan, think to yourself Bryan the Lion and visualize a lion. If you meet a guy named Bill, think of a dollar bill. You get the picture. You can also do it with verbal associations that connect to some detail about the person. For example, if you meet a woman named Sue and she's an attorney, remember "I'll sue you!" If you meet a guy named Ted and he has red hair, think of Red Ted.

This trick has served me well. Just last week, I was at a restaurant when Mark Victor Hansen, coauthor of the *Chicken Soup for the Soul* book series, walked by my table. I've had the privilege of meeting him in the past and being published in two his books. I called out, "Hey Mark!" as he strode by. He turned around and I asked, "How are you and Crystal doing?" He smiled and said, "Great!"

After leaving for a few minutes, he returned to my table with yet another person of notoriety, the famous artist Wyland, and introduced me to him. I have no doubt that my remembering his wife's name was part of what created the trust and rapport that prompted him to make the introduction, and I have since connected with both of them on social media. Of course, what Mark was not privy to was the image in my mind that helped me commit those names to memory: A "crystal" glass with a smudge "mark" on it!

Practice these tricks whenever you're out and about, meeting people. The best way to improve your memory is to use it. It will help with building relationships and keep your brain healthier at the same time!

#3

Always Be Opening

*You don't close a sale, you open a relationship if you
want to build a long-term, successful enterprise.*
Patricia Fripp

In the 1992 David Mamet film *Glengarry Glen Ross*, Alec Baldwin's character Blake, a hard-nosed, foul-mouthed real estate salesman, immortalized an old sales adage. In one of the movie's most memorable scenes, he writes on a blackboard the letters A-B-C. "Always Be Closing!" he yells at the salespeople he's been brought in to motivate.

"Only one thing counts in this life," he shouts, pacing the room and glaring at the figures slumped behind the desks. "Get them to sign on the line, which is dotted! You hear me, you *blankity blanks*?"

You get the idea, and I'm sure you can fill in the blanks. Now, as Blake is fond of saying, do I have your attention? Good, because I want to tell you something important. I'm going to tell you to do the *exact opposite* of the A-B-C. I call it the A-B-O, which stands for Always Be Opening. Yes, that's a counter-intuitive piece of advice for anyone in sales, but I'm an artist and thinking counter-intuitively is what I do.

Always Be Opening means to create relationships from a place of curiosity, free from agendas and available for possibilities you may not have even imagined. Because you know what? Your agendas are probably getting in the way of much bigger potential outcomes than you think you're looking for. Make room for the unexpected. Don't limit what may come from even the smallest connection with a stranger.

Disney teaches their employees—also known as cast members—to practice "passive listening." This means they are encouraged to eavesdrop on conversations with guests (with decorum, of course) in the hopes they may be able to intercede and help if any questions arise. This practice can be of value to you as well when you are out in social situations and can create great opportunities for openings! Just make sure that if you are in fact listening to one person, you give them your undivided attention even if you overhear something else happening behind you.

Always Be Opening means letting go of your sales quotas, your well-rehearsed pitches, and of course, your closes. Be open and stay open. Throw the doors wide and put a wedge under each one so they can't swing shut. Open means listening. Open means generous—focused not on what you want from the other person, but on what you can give to him or her. Henry Ford once said, "The man who will use his skill and constructive imagination to see how much he can give for a dollar, instead of how little he can give for a dollar, is bound to succeed." This same principle applies to sales and building relationships.

If you want to put this into practice right away, you can even take it literally. Open doors for people. That's right, actual doors. Open the door for someone at the grocery store or a restaurant, hold the elevator doors open for your co-worker, stick out your foot to open the train door for someone who's running to jump aboard (but don't forget to pull it back in before the door closes and the train leaves!). See if you can turn these physical "openings" into openings for conversation.

If you work in an office, leave your door open and say hi to everyone who passes or try throwing a paper airplane at them. Open your front door at home and sit out on the steps and greet whoever passes by.

Think about how you can create openings for connection every day. Openness is candy you can give to strangers. Forget about the close, the payoff, the signing on the dotted line. Trust me, that candy will come back to you, but probably not in the way you imagine it will. It will come back much sweeter than what you gave away. Coffee may be for closers, to borrow another of Blake's infamous lines, but candy is for openers.

#4

Make an Old Friend

*You know you must be doing something
right if old people like you.*
Dave Chappelle

She is so old that she was a waitress at the last supper. He is so old that his social security number is 1. Jokes like this are funny, but sometimes they discount the value that the "chronologically gifted" have to offer. If you want to develop the skill of talking and listening to strangers without looking for anything in return, here's a great way to practice: visit your local retirement home and make friends with some of the residents. I've done this several times and every time it surprises me. It is a great way to give some candy to people who will really appreciate it.

One of my recent retirement-home connections was a woman named Eunice. She was ninety-two years old, dressed to the nines, and full of life and energy. One question led to another, and I ended up talking to her for hours. She had been an aerial photographer during World War II and had the privilege of meeting General Douglas MacArthur. With six children, eighteen grandchildren, and several great-grandchildren, her legacy was rich and her wisdom deep. Many of the folks she now shared her life with came to her for advice, and she still had much to offer.

According to the Center for Disease Control, there are more than two million Americans living in nursing homes and residential care communities. Have you ever visited one? Many people say they find such places depressing, but I think they're quite the opposite. When you take the time to actually engage with people, these communities become uplifting places, and gold mines of life experience, wisdom, and great stories. Imagine how many people an average eighty-five-year-old has known throughout his or her lifetime. He or she may have been a leader in industry, a cop, a teacher, a parent, or even a celebrity. The fact is, older people have more to offer than most of us. We are all headed in that direction anyway, so we might as well get comfortable.

If you're concerned about seeming weird or creepy, don't worry; you can tell each person you meet exactly what you're doing so you won't seem like you have some hidden agenda. Just tell them, "I'm reading a book about connecting with strangers, and I'd love to hear your story." Being completely authentic and transparent is the best way to put other people at ease, as we'll discuss in #16.

When you arrive, find someone who's sitting alone in the lobby, the cafeteria, the garden, or the lounge, and strike up a conversation. Ask your friend-to-be to tell you his or her story. You will be amazed at what you learn. People in retirement homes today were born before 1950—in a completely different world! Just think about the changes they've seen in their lifetimes.

Here is a helpful strategy to get people to open up. Ask specific questions as opposed to general open-ended questions. For instance, instead of asking, "What did you do for a living?" ask, "When you were younger and starting out on your career path, what was the worst job you ever had?" From that perspective you will get more information, they will open up, and you will soon find out what they did for a living regardless. This approach also works with the other people you meet day-to-day, not just older folks. It gets people to turn back the wheels of their memory and opens doors for more conversation. People in general like to talk about themselves.

If you're still hesitating, here's another reason to try this: When you spend time socializing with these "old" friends, besides brightening up their day, you may even be contributing in some small way to their health and wellbeing. Researchers at the Harvard School of Public Health found evidence that elderly people in the United States who have an active social life may have a slower rate of memory decline, and may be less likely to develop dementia.[5] Now that's what I call friends with benefits!

#5

Get Your Ducks in a Flow

Chaotic action is preferable to orderly inaction.
Will Rogers

My front yard lacks the dark green manicured look that is so common in much of suburbia. This is thanks to a gaggle of geese (yes, a *gaggle*), a swan or two, and a badling (yes, a *badling*) of ducks, all munching and grazing to their hearts content. We live on a lake in sunny Southern California, which hosts a myriad of different waterfowl, with ducks being the main attraction. A big thank you goes to my lovely wife, Renée, who so earnestly feeds them cracked corn when I am not looking.

Sometime back, I gave up the fight of forever trying to keep my grass pristine when it became clear that I could not win. I can't even clean up the aftermath of their relentless grooming and fertilizing of my lawn. Now, as I cross my yard I just look up into the sky as to not see their handiwork, and hope that one of them does not decide to fly overhead at the same time and that I do not slip on their aforementioned handiwork.

Don't get me wrong, I love ducks. As a matter of fact, while in college I wrote a poem about ducks and even stopped traffic on a busy highway—putting my life at risk—to make way for a family of baby ducklings to cross. But I have learned one thing that is undeniable: it is impossible to control, manipulate, manage, or line up any ducks into a row.

Too many salespeople suffer from what I like to call Ducks in a Row Syndrome. They spend endless time planning, organizing, and strategizing, but avoid picking up the phone, ringing the doorbell, or getting out there and making connections. They spend so much time sharpening their pencils, designing their business cards, and refining their prospect lists that they have no time left to actually sell anything. Weeks, months, or even years later, they are still busy lining up their proverbial ducks, an exercise that, as I've already explained, is futile.

Planning and organizing (something I admit does not come easily to me) are certainly important components of any business. But, when it comes to creating and maintaining relationships, the most important thing you can do is take action. Move forward! Pick up the phone, go for a walk, talk to someone. ANYONE! Be creative. Be spontaneous. Creativity and spontaneity are heroic traits. Jump out of the plane and put your parachute on while you are on your way down.

Richard Branson, one of the world's best-known businessmen, credits his own success to the power of relationships and his willingness to move forward briskly. "Succeeding in business is all about making connections," he says. And his advice to others is unequivocal: "No matter how heavy your workload is, do not allow yourself to work in your cubicle or office all day, every day—for your own well-being and the health of your business, you need to get out and about, meeting people and developing relationships."[6]

Ducks in a Row Syndrome, or Analysis Paralysis, as it's sometimes known, has a simple cure: DO IT NOW! It's basic physics. Newton's law of inertia tells us that an object at rest will remain at rest unless acted on by an unbalanced force. An object in motion continues in motion with the same speed and in the same direction unless acted upon by an *unbalanced force*. In other words, if you sit at rest behind your desk, lining up your ducks, you're likely to stay that way indefinitely. But if you give yourself an initial push (an unbalanced force) and get out the door, you'll soon gain some momentum. And momentum translates as *feeling easier*.

You've probably experienced this yourself. Have you ever tried to push a stalled car? The initial push is the hardest, but once the car is rolling just a little it gains speed, then the pushing becomes much easier. Or think about a time when you were procrastinating on a particular project or task because the thought of actually doing it was so daunting; but when you finally got around to doing it, it turned out to be quite easy. Or maybe you've had the experience of standing on the edge of a high diving board hesitating to jump. That feeling of uneasiness becomes almost overwhelming—until you finally take the leap. Then it feels great! That is because you became the "unbalanced force." The first step in becoming the unbalanced force is to get up and get out there. The second step is to get up and get out there again, and again, and again. It's that simple! And it gets easier. Stop trying to get your ducks in a row, and get your ducks in a flow instead. Being in the "flow" or in the "zone" is what happens when you generate momentum, so that you start to feel like you're being carried. But you'll only get there if you get the ball rolling yourself. Push the car. Take the leap. Hold out your hand to a stranger.

A quote from the Kevin Costner baseball movie *Bull Durham* comes to mind. Skip, the quirky manager, played by the now-departed actor Trey Wilson, delivers this great line: "You guys, you lollygag the ball around the infield. You lollygag your way down to first. You lollygag in and out of the dugout. You know what that makes you? Lollygaggers!"

Stop lining up your ducks...and don't be a *lollygagger*!

Get out there today. Expose yourself to new people, places, and things. Don't fall into the trap of saying to yourself, "Tomorrow I'm going to go out and make ten new contacts. But today I'm going to do some research, make a list, get some new business cards printed, get a haircut, and pick up my good suit from the dry cleaner." If you do, you can pretty much guarantee that tomorrow your drive and enthusiasm will have dwindled to nothing, and you'll come up with a new list of ducks you need to line up before you can start. You'd be better off walking out into the street right now, without a list or a business card, with your hair a little long and whatever clothes you happen to be wearing, and giving some candy to the first five people you meet. Five real connections today are worth more than fifty well-behaved ducks. DO IT NOW!

#6

Know Your "Why"

Everyone has a purpose in life.
Perhaps yours is watching television.
David Letterman

When I was growing up, we would often visit Grandma's house for dinner. Being a farm girl from Oklahoma, my grandmother believed life would just not be the same without a hearty home-cooked meal. Her table was always heaped with all the fixin's you would expect: mashed potatoes, roast beef, gravy, carrot cake, rhubarb pie, sweet tea, you name it. Her cooking was the best, but luckily for my brother and me we played a lot of soccer to work off the heavy-duty cornucopia of calories!

Grandma took it as a personal affront if we did not finish every last bit of food on our plates and lick them clean enough to put right back in the cupboard. Before the table was cleared, she would look around, assess the situation, and decide if our plates were indeed cleaned to her satisfaction. If not, she would say, "Eat every Potato and Pea on your Plate."

My brother and I would laugh uncontrollably as she studiously went about the business of clearing the table with no regard as to the source of our hilarity. To this day, I am not quite sure whether that was her wit and humor or not. And I've never forgotten that early lesson about the importance of Ps.

These days, there are three Ps I value above all others (even the green kind—sorry, Grandma!). They are Passion, Purpose, and Persistence. Without the "Three Ps," nothing else can happen. As a matter of fact, nothing of greatness has ever been accomplished in the history of mankind without the Three Ps! And there have been many books written on the subject, so I won't belabor it here. However, I will simply say that before you trudge forth and start growing your business, it's critical that you know your "why." You need to know and be passionate about your purpose if you are to find the courage to be persistent enough to succeed.

Although the story below is not business related, it illustrates the point of how important and powerful knowing your "why" can be.

Many people ask themselves, *What will I do when I retire?* Well, *golf,* of course. For my cousin Bill Burke, this wasn't a very satisfying answer when he reached the ripe old age of sixty and contemplated the void of his newly opened schedule. He had already achieved many pinnacles throughout his long career in law: four Lifetime Achievement Awards, including one from the Business Law Section of the California State Bar Association.

"When I first retired," Bill told me, "I decided it was important to take up some kind of safe and sane hobby, like golf or tennis. After much thought and research, I settled on the sport of high-altitude mountaineering." Bill traveled to the Cascades and took a climbing course. Soon that seed grew to a strong passion for mountaineering and a rather "lofty" goal.

"After the class, I returned home and then immediately set off to climb Mt. Rainier in Washington. From there it was Mt. McKinley in Alaska, the highest mountain in the North America," he recalled. Soon, his passion and purpose called him to even greater heights. He determined to climb the legendary Mount Everest, the highest peak in the world. Bill's 3 Ps were tested to the limit on the day he was finally ready to go for the summit. He writes:

During the evening, the winds picked up, and, by morning, we were experiencing gale force winds. . . . This was what I had feared the most. After all the effort to get into position for a summit run, the weather was turning against me, threatening to put a violent and sad end to my dream of reaching the summit.

I stayed in my tent all day on May 22. There was no other option as the winds were now hurricane force, coming up the Southwest Face from Nepal, picking up speed as they crossed the South Col and roared down the Kangshung Face into Tibet on the other side. . . . I lay in my tent all day and into the evening, praying for better weather. . . .

Our plan was to head for the summit at 8 p.m. so we could summit before the unofficial 2 p.m. turnaround time the following day. Despite my prayers, the winds did not subside. They even got worse. At 8 p.m., my Sherpa, Mingma, entered my tent and recommended we delay our departure time until 10 p.m. I agreed. There was no surcease in the winds and, at 10 p.m., Mingma entered my tent again and asked, "We go up, or we go down? Up to you." Without any hesitation, I said, "We're moving up." My thinking was that, once we got off the South Col and started moving up the face of the mountain, the winds would be more tolerable. I was right.

Inside my tent, I slowly put on my climbing gear and then exited into the howling wind. I will never forget that moment. I looked up at the sky and could see billions of stars twinkling down in the blackness of the night, indifferent to my peril and my predicament. I felt as though I could reach out and touch them, and, in a strange sort of way, I was calmed. As I looked at the route up the Triangular Face to the South Summit, I could see the headlamps of the other climbers snaking up the mountain, each person completely detached from everyone else, frozen in his or her thoughts, dreams, fears, hopes, and aspirations.[7]

On May 23, 2009, at the age of sixty-seven, with frozen fingers and an oxygen mask, Bill Burke became the oldest American to reach the summit of Mt. Everest and return alive. His passion, purpose, and persistence had, quite literally, taken him to the top of the world.

Bill is the only person in history to climb the highest mountain on every continent after the age of sixty. His next goal, at the age of seventy-two, was to scale Mt. Everest again, only this time from the north side. On May 25, 2014, he accomplished this goal and became the oldest person outside Asia to climb Mt. Everest. Did I mention, he was seventy-two?

With passion, purpose, and persistence, you can move mountains—or, if you're as crazy as Bill, you may choose to climb them!

#7

Expect Failure

*Many of life's failures are people who did not realize
how close they were to success when they gave up.*
Thomas Edison

A common reason people hesitate when doing something that feels risky—like creating relationships with strangers—is the fear of failure. There's a good reason for that: you will fail from time to time. But that's okay. In order to hit the target, you have to throw a dart—a lot of darts. Some of your darts may land in the outer rings; others may even end up on the floor (or possibly in someone's forehead if you are not careful). So long as they don't hit anyone, keep throwing! The more you throw, the more likely you are to hit the bull's-eye.

As I write this, I am sitting beneath a large shady oak tree in the mountains above Palm Springs, California. I have left my home with its duck-ravaged lawn behind for a few days to focus on my book, and in place of my feathered friends, I now have squirrels to watch. Right now, several feet from my chair, there's a happy little squirrel I will call Ted. Okay, I can't claim to be able to recognize this particular squirrel among all the others, but the name seems to suit whichever squirrel happens to be gathering his harvest in my view at this moment. As a matter of fact, by the looks of him, I'd swear my wife has been secretly feeding the squirrels here as well.

As I observe Ted going about his business, I notice something very interesting. When he drops an acorn, he doesn't pound his furry little paw on his forehead and start sulking; he just keeps right on gathering. Clearly, Ted does not experience the same emotion of failure that we humans experience. To Ted there is no such thing as failure. He keeps on moving forward, whether he drops a few acorns or not. It also occurs to me that squirrels often "fail" to remember where they stash the hordes of acorns they collect—from which many more trees will grow and benefit others. So even their "failures" are blessings!

As I look back at my own life and consider some of the events that at the time I considered failures, I realize that they never ended up being quite as bad as I thought they were at the time. Invariably, if I hung in there, another door would open that I would not have even seen if the so-called failure had not happened. Can we all stand to learn a thing or two from my newfound friend Ted about failure?

As a creative individual, putting aside the fear of failure has been critical. I always start the creative process with the premise that "there's no such thing as a bad idea." This frees people from the fear of making a mistake or saying something stupid, and allows us to "brainstorm" freely. Here are a few other pointers that may help when it comes to creatively building relationships and get you over the fear of failure.

- You can't say the wrong thing to the right person.

- Don't assume the outcome of the conversation.

- Don't worry about what others may think. (See #15)

- Don't over analyze the situation before it has occurred.

- Don't worry about making mistakes (if you are not making mistakes occasionally, you are doing something wrong).

- Don't hesitate.

- Do listen, be friendly, and be empathic.

FUN FACTS

Famous, successful people fail too. Here are three of my favorite stories:

Mark Cuban, the billionaire owner of the NBA's Dallas Mavericks, became very wealthy when he sold his company to Yahoo for $5.9 billion. He has admitted that he was terrible at his early endeavors. His parents wanted him to have a normal job, so he tried carpentry but hated it. He was a short-order cook but a terrible one. He waited tables but couldn't open a bottle of wine with any effectiveness. When asked of his failures, he said, "I've learned that it doesn't matter how many times you fail; you only have to be right once. I was an idiot lots of times, but I learned from them all."

Michael Jordan is famous for being cut from his high school basketball team. He turned out to be one of the greatest basketball players ever. He never let failure deter him. In his words,

"I have missed more than 9,000 shots in my career. I have lost almost 300 games. On 26 occasions I have been entrusted to take the game-winning shot, and I missed. I have failed over and over and over again in my life. And that is why I succeed."

Thomas Edison. No list of success from failures would be complete without the man who gave us many inventions, including the light bulb. He knew failure wouldn't stop him and said, "If I find 10,000 ways something won't work, I haven't failed. I am not discouraged, because every wrong attempt discarded is another step forward."

#8

Play By the Two Rules

We think we understand the rules when we become adults, but what we really experience is a narrowing of the imagination.
David Lynch

If all this talk of spontaneity, creativity, and lack of preparation feels like it's going too far, don't worry. I'm not saying there aren't times when being strategic and being prepared are important. The trick, however, is not to let strategizing and preparing get in the way of taking action.

During my design days, I always had others working in the office with me. I craved the human interaction and creative collaboration that others brought to the table. When I interviewed people to work in my studio, I would look first and foremost at their attitude and drive and lastly at their experience and talent. Don't get me wrong; it's nice to have both. But I would much rather work with an eager soul willing to jump in and learn on the job than a talented prima donna with years of experience and all of his ducks in a row, who very often would also be stuck in a creative box—I refer to these people as "artsy-fartsies". This approach served me well, and I hired some great people who also become good friends. One such person was Robert Ball (or "Rawdirt" as my daughter Sara always called him.)

When Robert first visited my studio, green behind the ears, I remember telling him: "The first rule is there are no rules. And the second rule is that there are many rules." He looked at me with a puzzled frown. Channeling my best Yoda impersonation, all I said was, "You will soon understand."

What I didn't tell him at the time was that the line between the two rules is different for everyone. No, I'm not an oracle; I was merely trying to get him to think.

If you think about this yourself, you too will eventually discern which rules to follow and which ones to create for yourself, and particularly how they relate to relationship creation. It will depend, to some extent, on your own personal comfort zone (something we will explore further in #31). Of course, I am not talking about breaking the law—I am talking about breaking the rules of how you would normally do business, rules that have been set in place so long that experience leads you to take them for granted and not question them. I hope that while reading this book, you will make up some of your own rules as you go along, and that you'll be inspired to throw out a few rules as well.

In post–World War II Berlin, Germany, Colonel Gail Halvorsen, better known as the Candy Bomber, chose to break the rules and literally give candy to strangers. He is perhaps best known for his selfless acts toward others and is quoted as saying, "Service is the bottom line to happiness and fulfillment." It all began when he was flying supplies into Berlin, which was at that point under Soviet control, during the war. On one of his days off, while exploring the city, he saw thirty children lined up at Tempelhof airport, the main landing site for the airlift. These kids, he realized, had nothing without the aid of the U.S. troops. He reached in his pockets and pulled out some candy for the kids, wishing he had enough for all of them. He noticed how polite they were, not fighting over the candy, which was nowhere near enough to go around. At that moment, Halverson decided that he would come back in his plane and drop more candy for the kids. He gathered them round and explained his plan.

"How will we know which plane is yours?"

"I'll wiggle my wings," he replied. This earned him the nickname "Onkel Wackelflügel" or "Uncle Wiggly Wings."

Halverson returned to his base and used his ration to buy more candy, and also asked his friends to contribute. They created small parachutes out of extra clothes and handkerchiefs, and the next morning, when they flew in to make their regular supply drops, they also dropped boxes of candy attached to handkerchiefs. They did this once a week, and the children were very happy and began sending the parachutes back along with thank-you letters and artwork.

One day, Halverson was summoned to the office of his commanding officer. He was worried he'd gotten in trouble for breaking the rules, but it turned out to be quite the opposite. His commanding officer was very proud of his initiative. Ultimately, word of the candy-bombing reached Lieutenant General William H. Tunner, the commander of the airlift operation, which was known as Operation Vittles. He ordered Halverson's spontaneous gesture to be expanded into Operation "Little Vittles." As news found its way back to the United States, children all over the country began contributing candy, with candy-makers following suit shortly thereafter. By the end of the airlift, twenty-three tons of chocolate, chewing gum, and other candies had been dropped over various sites in Berlin. And none of that would have happened, had not Gail Halverson broken the rules in order to give some candy to some small strangers.

Think of a rule, any rule (it doesn't matter which), and write it down. It may be something as simple as "Don't Take Candy from Strangers." Now consider the ramifications of breaking that rule and write those down. Then mix them up, turn them around and reswizzle them, rethink them. Now look at that rule again and see what new rule you come up with.

PART 2

Nurturing Your Existing Relationships

Do you remember the old song from grade school that went: "Make new friends but keep the old. One is silver and the other's gold"? That may sound a bit elementary, but it's the truth. As you make new friends and acquaintances, it's also important to continue nurturing your existing relationships. And don't assume you know your longstanding friends. Bring as much curiosity and openness to your oldest friendship as you bring to a first meeting with a stranger.

This section offers some suggestions for ways to keep track of your existing network, re-energize your connections with old and new friends, and stay connected as time goes by. These are principles that will also apply to any new friends or acquaintances you make as a result of putting the advice in this book into practice. After all, your existing friends were strangers once, and people who are strangers today could be friends tomorrow. Silver or gold, your connections are your most valuable assets.

Without friends no one would choose to live,
though he had all other goods.
Aristotle

#9

Be Friendfull

I get by with a little help from my friends.
The Beatles

If you're old enough to have been a fan of the sitcom *I Love Lucy*, you may remember the episode where everyone seemed to have forgotten Lucy's birthday. Lucy, played by the red-haired maven of comedy Lucile Ball, gets so depressed at her friends' apparent obliviousness to her special day that she wanders around town aimlessly, sulking and sad. She ends up in the city park and meets the "Friends of the Friendless," a group of likeminded, downtrodden friendless people. Lucy joins the ranks of this unhappy mob as all of them march together to her husband Ricky Ricardo's nightclub, The Tropicana, to protest the neglect of their newfound member.

"We are friends of the friendless, yes we are, yes we are. We are friends of the friendless, be they near, be they far," they sing in unison as they march. "We are here for the downtrodden, and we sober up the sodden. We are friends of the friendless, yes we are, yes we are."

Arriving at the club with her new comrades, Lucy gives a speech in front of the whole crowd. She tells them that today she has learned the true meaning of friendship.

"These people are my friends," she declares. "The Friends of the Friendless! And I was friendless. I was just a bit of flotsam in the sea, a pitiful outcast, shunned by my fellow man. I was a mess. The people I thought were my friends forsook me. Even my own husband proved he was just a 'husband,' and not a friend. Today was my birthday, and do you think anybody remembered? Nobody remembered! Nobody did a thing about it. Nobody even as much as... not a single..."

Before she can finish her tear-jerking speech, Lucy is shocked to find that what she has walked into was in fact a surprise party—for her!

The irony of the situation is, of course, in the title of the group. All of the Friends of the Friendless were considered friends by the mere fact that they belonged together to the Friends of the Friendless. Lucy made a whole new group of friends just by going out to the park and talking to strangers—and she also misread the feelings of her existing friends. Which gets to my point: Who are your friends and how well do you know them? And, who are the friends of your friends? What is a friend? Is it possible that you have more friends than you might realize?

You might be thinking, *No, not me.* Perhaps you're one of those people who wanders the park feeling friendless and alone. But even you probably have more friends than you think. This book is focused on creating new relationships, but I don't mean for you to do so at the expense of your existing ones. So before we get out in the street and start giving candy to strangers, let's take a moment to look through your mental Rolodex (or your Contacts app for those of you from the younger persuasion) and start making a map.

You can do this on a large whiteboard, on a wall using Post-it notes, or just on a big piece of paper. Put a dot in the middle marked "Me" and then start writing the names of all your friends in a big circle around it. Once you've exhausted the names that come to mind, look at the ones you've written and ask yourself, *How did I meet him or her?* This will probably spark a whole lot more names. Then ask, *Has he or she introduced me to anyone else?* You may be amazed at how many names you come up with. You may also start to think about how many of these friends were once strangers. There's nothing like making a map of your network to remind you of the value of connectedness.

FUN FACT

International Friendship Day is a day for celebrating friendship, if you didn't deduce that by the name. Friendship Day celebrations occur on different dates in different countries. In the United States, it occurs on the first Sunday in August. However, some cities, such as Oberlin, Ohio, celebrate Friendship Day with their own date.

Friendship Day was originally proposed by Joyce Hall, the founder of Hallmark Cards, in 1930 (it was also generally promoted by the National

Association Greeting Card Association during the 1920s). Initially it was met with resistance, being that it was too commercial of a gimmick, designed to promote greetings cards. By the 1940s the number of Friendship Day cards in the United States had dwindled and the holiday all but died out. However, it has been revitalized in Asia, where several countries celebrate it every year. Whether you live in the United States or abroad, Friendship Day is a great way to remind yourself of the friends in your own life—but don't wait all year to do something about it! By following the tips in this book, you can make every day Friendship Day.

#10

Track Your Tribe

*Ultimately, we actually all belong
to only one tribe, to Earthlings.*
Jill Tarter, *Astronomer*

I have a client with whom I have worked with for over twenty years, but I have never met him in person. He lives less than two hours' drive from my studio. I am not proud of this, yet I know a lot about him and consider him a friend. As I write, I have made a commitment to myself to visit him in person this year and hand him a copy of this book. No amount of virtual connection can substitute for an in-person meeting, however brief.

Do you know where your friends live? These days, when so many of us are connected virtually through social media, it's easy to have no idea where our so-called friends physically reside. If you're only relating over the Internet, maybe that doesn't matter. But if you travel, you may be missing opportunities to connect with the people in your social networks and turn virtual connections into actual friendships or business.

The good news is, there are plenty of tools out there that can help you to "track your tribe," so that when you travel you can connect with your friends in person. Take the time to find out where people live so that you never arrive in a strange city without already knowing you have friends in town.

If you're a smartphone user, there are several apps you can use that will show you your contacts and social media friends on a map. Just search for "social mapping apps." Social networks like Facebook will also let you search your friends by their current city. And if you're an old-school type, you can still track your tribe. Scroll through your Rolodex to find out where your friends live, then buy a big map and put pins in it.

When I travel to a new city for an event or speaking engagement, I always make a point to make a new friend in that city. Although I may sometimes have used Facebook as a tool to connect before the fact, I also enjoy the spontaneity of meeting new people while I am in a particular city, and then knowing that when I revisit that city in the future, I have a local friend as well as a hub of influence for my business.

Make it a policy never to travel without seeing at least one old friend and making one new one.

#11

Play Rolodex Roulette

*The greatest irony is that people with Rolodexes
are no longer LinkedIn. And if that pun doesn't
make sense, don't ask anyone in your
Rolodex to explain it.*
Ryan Lilly

Okay, I realize I am aging myself with the title of this tip. You may not be old enough to have ever owned a Rolodex; perhaps you don't even know what one is. But "Contacts App Roulette" doesn't sound so good, so I'll stick with my old-fashioned version. The game works either way.

It goes like this. Once a week, randomly select someone from among your connections, either by closing your eyes and opening your Rolodex or by clicking blindly on a contact. No matter who that person is (assuming it's someone you like; if not, why is he or she in your Rolodex?), reach out to him or her. Pick up the phone, write an e-mail, send a text—and make it personal. Ideally, you'll have been staying in touch with the important developments in your friends' lives (see #14 for more on how to do this) so you can mention the person's new job, new marriage, new baby, new goldfish, and so on (or not mention the ex-wife, as the case may be.)

Sometimes, all that will happen is a simple exchange of e-mails, but if it's someone local, you might be able to take him to lunch or buy her a coffee. You never know where it might lead. And it's surprising how often you will find that you reach out to someone and she says, "You know, I was just thinking about you!" We all have those random thoughts about people we rarely stay in touch with, but so few people actually take the extra step and pick up the phone. Be the one who does.

Also, include some candy! Bring a small playful or thoughtful gift if you meet in person. Send a link to something the person might be interested in if you're communicating by e-mail or on social media. We'll talk more about how to do this in #43.

Play Rolodex Roulette at least once a week, and I guarantee you'll feel more connected to your existing network than you have in years, and it will feel like you are taking action! Who knows where those simple re-connections will lead.

FUN FACTS

The name Rolodex comes from a combination of the words *rolling* and *index*. It was invented by Arnold Neustadter and Hildaur Neilsen in Brooklyn, New York, in 1956. Store owners were initially skeptical about the appeal of this strange device, but by the 1980s there was one on almost every desk. A full Rolodex became an important status symbol—some models held up to 6,000 cards. Lawsuits were filed against employees who left their jobs and took their Rolodexes with them. In fact, an entire episode of the 1980s hit show *Moonlighting* was devoted to a story about a stolen Rolodex that was being held ransom for $50,000. These days, many of us have transferred our precious contacts to digital devices, but the name *Rolodex* lives on as a general term to describe the sum total of an individual's accumulated business contacts. And yes, I still have one.

#12

Make Contagious Connections

Eventually everything connects—people, ideas, objects.
The quality of the connections is the key to quality per se.
Charles Eames

Have you ever heard someone say, "He's connected"? I recently met Larry Benet who Forbes calls one of the most connected men in America. That's pretty connected!

What is the average number of people with whom one individual can maintain stable social relationships? Of course, the word "stable" is a very gray area here, if you know what I mean, but putting that aside for a moment, there are people who have proposed answers to this question. The most widely accepted is known as "Dunbar's number" after the British anthropologist Robin Dunbar, who found a correlation between primates' brain size and the size of their social groups. He posited that the number is around 150, and showed persuasive evidence that this has been true since the time of the earliest hunter-gatherer human ancestors who shared our brain size. Now that brings new meaning to the term monkey business.

Other numbers have been suggested, but Dunbar's estimate remains one of the more widely accepted. So let's assume you have a circle of friends and acquaintances that includes about 150 people. The exciting news is that each of these people also has a similar circle. Of course, there may be some overlap, particularly with your close friends who may share many of the same connections, but nevertheless, you could be "one degree of separation" away from as many as 20,000 people!

One of the keys to growing your network and tapping into the power of relationships is to make your connections "contagious." That means making everyone you meet a stepping-stone to a new connection. Of course, I mean this in the figurative sense, not the literal.

I'm sure you have probably heard someone tell a story and say, "My friend's sister's aunt's neighbor has a cousin who works with a guy that..." And others listening then roll their eyes at the degree of vagueness of the connections just rattled off. My mind, by contrast, starts to whirl with the connectedness of the people. I visualize all of the people and how they relate to one another (and yes, I listen to the story too). The point is not that I necessarily do anything with that information; it's that I have trained myself to think non-linearly and to connect the dots.

If you want your friends to introduce you to their friends, you need to let them know it! People won't necessarily assume that you want to meet new people. Tell your friends you'd love to meet their friends. Or you might throw a party for some of your friends and ask each person to bring along at least one person you don't know.

In business, of course, these friend-of-friend connections are known as "referrals." When I was running my design business, I would always ask my clients, friends, family, and business associates if they had any referrals or knew of anyone who might be interested in my services. This kind of "word-of-mouth advertising" is powerful for two reasons. First, it expands your circle of connections, and second, people are more likely to buy from a friend's referral than otherwise.

Make your existing connections contagious, and before you know it, you'll be connecting to friends of friends of friends...

#13

Count Your Bacon

*I joke that my epitaph will be, "No Oscars,
but at least he had a game named after him."*
Kevin Bacon

Dwight Stones is a two-time Olympic bronze medalist and former three-time world record holder in the men's high jump who won nineteen national championships during his sixteen-year career. Stones raised the world high jump record to seven feet seven inches in 1976 and added another quarter inch to the record two months later. In 1984, he became the first athlete to both compete and announce at the same Olympic Games. Since then, he has been a commentator for all three major television networks in the United States and abroad and continues to cover track and field on television.

Back in the ninth grade, my friend Jim Tyler and I would ride our banana-seated Schwinn bicycles up to the "high jump pit" at California State University, Long Beach to practice our fledgling jumping skills. One day when we arrived, we were confronted by a tall, slender gentleman who had already been practicing and using the pit. I say confronted, because, as he was deep in thought and concentration, and preparing to once again sail gracefully over the high bar, our quiet murmurs of awe and amazement must have been not so quiet to him—and he wasn't shy about letting us know as much.

We then realized *who* we were watching and getting "coached" by. It was the great Olympic high jumper, Dwight Stones. We were honored to have been reprimanded by such a legend! Even now, when I watch ABC Sports and see Dwight colorfully commentating on my TV, I talk in a hushed whisper.

About four years later, fresh out of high school on my first day at Long Beach City College, I was walking across a footbridge when another student stopped me and said, "Hey, I know you. You're that guy that high jumps! What's your name? Oh yeah, Dwight Stones! Can I have your autograph?" I was dumbfounded. So I gave him *my* autograph.

First of all, aside from our similar height, I looked nothing like Dwight Stones with his blond hair and Nordic features, nor could I jump as high, even in my prime. And I happen to be ten years younger than him, I might add. I am still not quite sure what transpired that day, but I seemed to be destined to keep crossing paths with Mr. Stones.

A couple of years ago, I found out that Dwight lived only a few miles away from me and coached high jump to the up and coming stars of track and field in our area. Of course, I went to watch and visit him, and we have stayed in touch ever since. Since then, I also discovered that we have a few friends in common, one of whom is Ron Brown, an Olympic champion in his own right (in addition to being an NFL star). All of this running into Dwight, both directly and indirectly over the years, made me think, *How connected are we to anyone? And who are the people we are connected to, connected to? How can we connect the dots from one person to another?*

You've probably heard the popular theory of "Six Degrees of Separation." Originated in 1929 by Hungarian author Frigyes Karinthy, the theory posits that any two people on earth are only six or fewer acquaintances apart from one another. That means that if you want to connect to anyone in the world, you can get there through no more than six "friend of a friend" connections. There have been numerous logistical, mathematical, and statistical studies rendered about this theory, and it has inspired many books, several movies, and various other creative expressions, of which none are quite such fun as "The Six Degrees of Kevin Bacon."

This is a parlor game, wherein movie buffs challenge each other to find the shortest path between an arbitrary actor and the prolific Hollywood character actor Kevin Bacon. It rests on the assumption that any individual involved in the Hollywood film industry can be linked through his or her film roles to Kevin Bacon within six steps. The number of steps is known as the person's "Bacon number." Hence, Bacon himself has a Bacon number of 0, his co-stars are 1, and so on. I personally have a Bacon number of 2.

The game was created in early 1994 by three Albright College students, Craig Fass, Brian Turtle, and Mike Ginelli, who claim they came up with the idea when watching the Kevin Bacon movie *Footloose*. When the film ended, on came another Bacon movie, *The Air Up There*, and they began to speculate about how many movies Bacon had been in and how many people he must have worked with. They managed to get the media interested in their game and appeared on several major TV shows with Bacon himself explaining the concept. The actor has since appeared in several commercials built around the idea, including one for Visa and one for the 4G cell phone network in the UK, and his name has become almost synonymous with connectedness.

I have often wondered whether any of the strangers I have run into were really only once removed by a friend in common. Or, if any of those strangers were really friends from childhood who I grew apart from and, therefore, didn't recognize. I recently found out that one of the distributors in my sales organization, with whom I have been working for over three years, is actually a cousin of mine from Iowa! Yes, it really is a small world.

Experiment with the "six degrees" principle in your own network. Think of someone you'd like to meet and see if you can connect the dots to get to them. Or think about your existing friends and who they might know. Count your bacon, and you may even find that it helps you bring home the bacon!

As we'll discuss in #45, social networks like LinkedIn are great tools for doing this. And as you go about building connections, remember that no one is really a stranger. At the most, they're a friend of a friend of a friend of a friend of a friend of a friend. Wouldn't it be fun to introduce a friend to a stranger and say, "Suzanne, I'd like you to meet a friend of a friend of a friend of a friend of a friend of a friend of mine, George."

FUN FACT

Kevin Bacon has worn the cloak of his celebrity quite graciously and with humor. Expounding on the notoriety of the six degrees concept that his name has garnered, Bacon has created a website for people with causes to connect with celebrities. Are you a grassroots organizer, a church leader, a volunteer—somebody who wants to make a difference in your neighborhood or town? His site will connect you with celebrities to build media buzz around your cause. Check out www.sixdegrees.org.

#14

Don't Let Your Friends Grow Up to be Strangers

True friendship is like sound health; the value
of it is seldom known until it be lost.
Charles Caleb Colton

The English poet T.S. Eliot wrote a wonderfully stirring poem called *The Cocktail Party,* in which he points out that people are forever changing: "What we know of other people/Is only our memory of the moments/During which we knew them." He goes on to suggest, "We must also remember/That at every meeting we are meeting a stranger." I love this idea, as it reminds us to keep our friendships fresh—even those that are most enduring. And of course, I would also say the opposite: that at every meeting, even with a stranger, we are meeting a potential friend.

I recently attended a funeral for the wife of longtime friend. Although it would have been better under different circumstances, it was nice to see him and my other friends from the same group and reconnect. It brought to mind that we needed to connect more often so as not to see each other only at funerals. I came up with the idea for all of us to go camping together and plant a tree *in memoriam* to all of our friends and family we have lost along the way.

If you recognize that your friends are always changing, you'll understand why it's important to keep up to date on the important events in their lives. Otherwise they will become strangers to you, and you'll find yourself in that awkward situation where you meet an old friend at a party and ask how his work is going, unaware that he joined a dude ranch and became a cowboy (for those of you who have seen the great buddy movie *City Slickers*). Here are some suggestions for making sure your friends don't become strangers:

- Use social media to stay in touch with your friends' lives and interests even when you don't see them very often. Check their job status on LinkedIn and look at their posts on Facebook or Twitter. This way you'll reconnect quicker when you do get together. (See Part 7 for more tips on how to use social media.)

- Send personalized notes by e-mail or mail at Christmas or New Year's. These holidays are a great opportunity to reconnect with old friends, so don't waste them by sending mass e-mails. It doesn't take long to write a few personal lines, but it goes a long way. Include a few broad questions: Where are you working these days? How's your family? What's been the most significant thing that happened for you this year? This way, you invite the other person to send you a quick response and they'll tell you the important details you need to know.

- With new friends, connections, and acquaintances, keep a short journal of notes about them in your computer. Then, when you speak to them next and you happen to have remembered the name of their pet goldfish, Rhonda, they will feel honored and they will most certainly remember you. In this vein, Richard Branson says he carries a notebook with him when he meets with people who work for his companies around the world so he can jot down inspiring stories or ideas that people mention. "As well as being a great launching pad for new collaborations, these notes help me remember what we last spoke about, and I can ask how their business idea is developing," he says. "Building meaningful business relationships is very important, as people are a company's biggest asset. Remembering anything I have in common with somebody and the context of our last meeting helps cut through the chit-chat when we next meet and become better friends."[8]

- Another great way to stay connected with friends is to enter their birthdays into your smartphone or computer. However, also enter a date exactly two months prior to their actual birthday and schedule a reminder. That way you can be reminded to call them for something other than their birthdays and still remember when their birthdays are!

The key point of this book is that getting to know strangers is a great way to meet new friends and grow your business—but don't forget about your existing friends along the way.

PART 3

Overcoming Common Obstacles to Connection

Think about going out and talking to a stranger and I'm sure your mind fills with excuses why it's not such a good idea. We all have plenty of very good reasons why we feel it's not safe, not smart, not polite, not necessary, and so on. In this section, I'll address some of the most common obstacles we present ourselves with, and suggest some ways you might get around, over, or under them—or just realize they weren't real in the first place.

Remember, your perspective and attitude is everything. Do you see obstacles as roadblocks or as stepping stones? Even better, treat obstacles as though they are nothing more than dumbbells at the gym, making you stronger every time you use them.

He that is conscious of a stink in his breeches,
is jealous of every wrinkle in another's nose.
Benjamin Franklin, *Poor Richard's Almanack*

#15

Forget About What
Others Think

*If you gotta be wrong 'bout somthin', that's 'bout
the best thing they is to be wrong 'bout.*
Walt Kelly, *cartoonist*

"What other people think of you is none of your business."

You may have heard variations on this statement over the years, and no one seems quite sure who first spoke those words of wisdom, but one thing is for certain: they are wise words indeed.

Most of us spend an inordinate amount of time worrying about what other people think of us. When it comes to connecting with strangers, the biggest obstacle is usually our ideas and fears about what they think of us. Get over it! I've often heard bestselling author and pastor Rick Warren say, "Whatever you think others think about you, you're probably wrong anyway." Your own imagination is usually far more harshly critical than anyone else would be. The things you imagine others think about you are much worse than what they are likely to actually be thinking. So let's just assume you're wrong, or you're at least exaggerating. And right or wrong, I firmly believe that as the old saying goes, it's none of your business.

Worrying about what others will think is a surefire way to talk yourself out of ever taking the risk of saying hello to a stranger, let alone making a new friend. Whenever you catch yourself doing this, just tell yourself firmly, "It's none of my business."

#16

Unmask Yourself

*"I quite agree with you," said the Duchess; "and the moral of
that is—'Be what you would seem to be'—or if you'd like
it put more simply—'Never imagine yourself not to be
otherwise than what it might appear to others that
what you were or might have been was not
otherwise than what you had been would
have appeared to them to be otherwise.'"*
Lewis Carroll, *Through the Looking Glass*

My friend Tim is a clown. I say this with the utmost respect and admiration because he was a genuine bona fide clown, back in the 1980s, for Ringling Brothers and Barnum and Bailey Circus. He even went to clown school to learn the nuances of clowning, or at least to learn what didn't already come naturally to him. Yes, there really is a clown school. Over 60,000 hopeful clown candidates apply every year for this prestigious twelve-week course. However, only sixty are hand-picked to be a part of this special and exclusive club, where they learn the fine art of pie throwing and the timing of a well-placed banana peel slip, how to juggle, how to walk on stilts, and how to earn a thunderous guffaw from a crowd.

Now, as a professional humorist and writer, Tim is a clown of a different sort—a comedy historian, standup comic, and all-around funny guy. As prolific a writer of jokes as there ever was, if you ask him for ten gags, he will come back with fifty. Having been a member of Jonathan Winters' roundtable breakfast for writers, he also wrote for Pat Paulsen, who once ran for president. He carries in his wallet a great keepsake given to him by Eleanor Keaton, wife of the late and great comic Buster Keaton, who some would say is the greatest physical comedian (and comedy director) of all time.

"Eleanor was so sweet and kind," Tim recalled, "and the opportunity to reminisce with the wife one of our most quintessential clowns was so impactful. She shared with me Buster's thoughts on the comedy of his day and on his getting sober and how the clown in him, back then, was effortless and free. To this day, I still have in my wallet a blank check she gave me, with her address and phone number on it. It's my reminder to be great, to strive, and to remain true to who I am."

However, if there is one thing I know that I learned from Tim, it's that many clowns are not always who they appear to be on stage. Behind the face paint, rubber noses, overinflated shoes, and squirting lapel flowers, clowns are often very different people than their stage personas.

When I was about nine years old, my Uncle Jack would come into town and take all of us to the circus. A line of elephants, trunk to tail, would slowly parade down the middle of Pine Avenue in Long Beach, California, on their way to the big top tents, while a small man wearing all black scurried about behind them with a very large shovel. And trailing them, the best part: a dozen clowns all stuffed inside a single Volkswagen Bug, with faces, elbows, and butts all pressed firmly against every window.

I looked forward to this event every year with bated breath, but at that age my understanding of the world did not include the reality of who those people actually were behind their bright colored costumes, much less the understanding that they were real people with their own lives.

I learned later, listening to Tim's stories, of the lonely nights traveling on the circus train among the other clowns. Each of them had their own issues, desires, and dysfunctions, and many of them were quite sad and lonely people.

As human beings, we are all clowns, whether figuratively or literally. The face paint we show the world is often very different from our authentic inner selves. When meeting strangers, it's tempting to put on a mask, a face that looks more confident or successful than your own. It's tempting to paint on a big sunny smile and hide your eyes behind some big glasses. But if you do this, you'll only invite other people to wear their masks too. And you'll create another obstacle to really connecting, because you'll constantly be worried about upholding the image you've created, making sure your mask doesn't slip. You'll be concerned that the other person might glimpse the real you, and you're convinced the real you is not interesting or funny or successful enough. You'll be afraid of being unmasked, which will make you unavailable for what's possible in that moment of connection.

Authenticity is one of the most powerful things you can bring to a new connection. Unmask yourself, be genuine and transparent, and you'll free yourself from the need to worry about anyone else unmasking you. You'll have all of your energy and attention available for listening to the other person and getting to know him or her. And you're much more likely to meet another authentic person, because when you unmask yourself, you invite others to leave their masks at home as well. Be yourself, whoever you are. People would rather meet you than your painted face, however bright and beautiful your clown smile is.

FUN FACTS

In clown school, clown cadets take a pie-throwing class, in which they are taught to hurl shaving-cream-filled pies in such a way as to make cleaning up more efficient. After all, an elephant slipping on a pie is not all that funny (maybe a little?), and with two to three shows a day, expediency for the next show is always part of the job. Pie throwing is a very serious skill to master. A well-placed pie in the face is a funny thing, but breaking the nose of one of your fellow clowns is not.

One area of professional clownery that I find very intriguing, and something you should ponder, is how clowns work a crowd. If a clown performs what is called a "108"—this is a technical term for a very large slip where both legs fly vertically into the air, then said clown lands flat onto his or her back hopefully with a loud thump—and does not look at the crowd, it is nothing more than acrobatics. But, if he or she does a 108 while looking out into the eyes of the audience, that is something entirely different. The first is merely an act and the other is an "act of comedy." The clowns that do their job the best "relate" to the audience by communicating directly either through physical or verbal actions as opposed to just going through the motions like an athlete.

#17

Invite People to Laugh at You

*Whoever undertakes to set himself up as a judge
of truth and knowledge is shipwrecked
by the laughter of the gods.*
Albert Einstein

Ella Wheeler Wilcox wrote a poem called *Solitude*, which begins: "Laugh, and the world laughs with you/Weep, and you weep alone/For the sad old earth must borrow its mirth/But has trouble enough of its own."

I say that if you can help a stranger to laugh, even if it's at your own expense, you are halfway to making a friend.

One of the most common fears I hear when I suggest talking to strangers is "people will laugh at me." We're terrified of not being taken seriously, of appearing ridiculous or looking stupid. Of course, it's highly unlikely that strangers will laugh at you for saying hello. Remember, your worst fears are probably wrong. But just in case, here's a great strategy for dealing with the fear of other people laughing at you—laugh at yourself first, and then invite them to laugh with you.

Being self-deprecating is a great way to break the ice. Used appropriately, this style can help to establish trust. Poking fun at yourself can be seen as proof that you are open, honest, humble, and don't take yourself too seriously. The trick with this kind of humor is not to take it too far, or people will think your self respect meter is a little low.

#18

Sell Your Story

Great stories happen to those who can tell them.
Ira Glas

The lights had been turned back up, the spotlight was off, and my presentation was over. The storm of applause had finally faded, and the audience began filing out. I breathed a sigh of relief. A big sigh. Public speaking, at that point in my life, was not exactly something that I jumped out of bed in the morning, clicking my heels together, to go do.

An hour earlier, I hadn't known how I would get to this point. I'd been standing on the stage in front of the very large crowd when my carefully ordered index cards with all my notes suddenly slid from the podium and cascaded to the floor as though a magician were performing the ol' fifty-two-card pick-up trick. I had a momentary flashback to a grade-school play when I had forgotten to prepare, didn't know my lines, and panicked so badly I ran off the stage.

Nope, not this time, I said to myself. I have never had the pleasure of skydiving, but I am sure I must have felt a similar adrenaline rush. I left my cards on the floor, where they seemed to want to be, and walked out from behind the podium to the center of the stage, naked and unrehearsed (well, actually I had on a very nice suit, but I might as well have been in my birthday suit).

I told my story. The story that I have lived and breathed. A story of passion, pain, purpose and triumph. I spoke from the heart about how I'd come to be standing there that day. I held nothing back—I relived it all on stage. It felt as though I was soaring above the crowd. I told them about how my mother committed suicide when I was fourteen, and many years later, my brother and a good friend did the same. I told them how I'd struggled to rise above these tragedies, how I'd stumbled and gotten up again, how I'd faced bankruptcy and struggled with addiction, but had come out smiling. Later, a few people came forward and told me that the talk I gave that day was one of the best they ever witnessed. But the most powerful response came from a stranger who approached the stage as everyone else was beginning to file out of the auditorium.

He shook my hand and told me: "This morning I was looking at a handful of sleeping pills and a bottle of vodka. Two weeks ago I lost my job and came home to an empty house only to find out that my wife had left me and taken the kids. With that, on top of my health issues, my world has crumbled. I wasn't going to come and see you speak today, but something told me that I should. Maybe it was God—I think that it was. I am very grateful that I did. Stan, after hearing your story and seeing your passion, your drive, your spiritual commitment, and how you have turned things around, I have hope that I can turn things around too. Thank you. You saved my life today."

He broke down crying, gave me a hug, then turned and walked away through the crowd. I stood there, teary-eyed and without words, and watched him disappear through the back door of the auditorium. From that day I learned to never underestimate the power of your story.

One of my mentors, Isaac Waksul, used to say something that has always stuck with me: "You have to move people to move business." In the business of relationships, your story is your currency and the best way to "move" people. Everyone loves a good story—that's why humans have been telling them ever since our prehistoric ancestors gathered around their campfires.

A story is one of the most effective ways you can connect with people. When you learn how to weave stories into your conversations, message, product, or business, you will find that the connections you make with people will happen much quicker. I'm not saying you should consider every person you meet to be a captive audience for the long version of your autobiography. But knowing your own story—practicing it, honing it, choosing the most powerful points (notice that I did not say PowerPoint, which is the antithesis of a good story) and knowing how to deliver them with great impact—is a powerful tool for making connections. The story

I just shared is perhaps my most powerful example, but I've had countless other situations where simply sharing my story—sometimes just the one-minute or the five-minute version—has forged a surprising and instantaneous connection with a stranger.

Okay, you may be thinking, *Maybe that's true in social settings, but what about when I'm trying to do business? Surely my prospective clients or partners don't want to hear my life story?* Well, you'd be surprised. These days, some of the most successful businesses are realizing that storytelling is an untapped resource, and they're scrambling to learn how to do it better.

There is a well-known saying that "people buy from people they know, like, and trust." Stories can connect us to our listeners, our customers, or our clients, in a very powerful way that builds trust. When you share your own real-life stories or the stories of others, it helps other people to feel that they have gotten to know you as an authentic person. Authentic people who have struggled with problems and who have figured out how to overcome them are attractive and more trustworthy to others! That's not to say that your story has to involve a tragedy (it can also include humor, as we'll discuss in Part 5), but all great stories have some sort of conflict and then a resolution.

These days, we even have the science to prove it. According to Harrison Monarth, author of the article "The Irresistible Power of Storytelling as a Strategic Business Tool," in *Harvard Business Review:*

"Storytelling evokes a strong neurological response. Neuroeconomist Paul Zak's research indicates that our brains produce the stress hormone Cortisol during the tense moments in a story, which allows us to focus, while the cute factor of the animals releases oxytocin, the feel-good chemical that promotes connection and empathy. Other neurological research tells us that a happy ending to a story triggers the limbic system, our brain's reward center, to release dopamine which makes us feel more hopeful and optimistic."[9]

(Ironically, the product I was speaking about when I shared my story that day is clinically proven to lower Cortisol.)

The specific words you use when you tell your story can also have great impact.

Science writer Matthew McDonald shares this example in his book *Your Brain: The Missing Manual:*

A single descriptive word can manipulate how the mind remembers an event. For example, in a 1974 experiment, 45 people watched the film of a car accident. Different groups of people were asked how fast the cars were going using different trigger words, such as "hit," "smashed," "collided," bumped," and "contacted." The group whose question included the word "smashed" estimated the cars were going 10 mph faster than the group whose word was "contacted." A week later, when participants were asked about broken glass, those who were asked more forceful trigger words reported that there was broken glass even though there was none.[10]

Michael Margolis, author of *Believe Me* and founder of Story University, notes that, "People don't really buy a product, solution, or idea, they buy the story that's attached to it."[11] Tom Durrell, former CIO of Blue Cross Blue Shield, says, "When you're conversing with coworkers, customers, or investors, the richness and meaning of your story is what people really buy."[12]

In his book *Tell to Win*, Peter Guber explains that telling a great story can often mean the difference between success and failure. Knowing this, he was able to motivate, persuade, and influence many people and hold the company together as the CEO of Sony Pictures Entertainment, while they were going through a difficult adjustment period.

You don't just have to tell stories. Ask other people to share *their* stories! You will find that when you encourage someone else to tell their own story, most will be eager to do so and this in turn will move the conversation forward.

The hugely popular blog "Humans of New York" is a great example of how powerful this is. Started as a photo blog in 2010 by Brandon Stanton after he lost his job, it was initially going to be a series of portraits of strangers Stanton met on the streets of New York City. Then he started asking each of his subjects to tell their story, and the blog quickly went viral. Check it out for yourself at www.humansofnewyork.com. I challenge you to read ten stories and remain unmoved. More than twelve million people follow Stanton's posts on Facebook today, and the blog has inspired major philanthropic action as well. Just remember that the next time you wonder if someone is really interested in the story of a stranger.

#19

Rehearse Your Story

Everything is practice.
Pelé

Most would agree that Edson Arantes do Nascimento, better known as Pelé, was one of the greatest soccer players and all around athletes of all time. I love his quote above for several reasons, not least of which is that I played soccer as a small boy and all the way up to semi-pro as an adult. But also because Pelé understood what it meant to practice both on and off the field. When he wasn't playing, he used everyday situations to prepare, think, and strategize about his next game. It may sound clichéd, but Pelé knew that practice really does make perfect.

When it comes to telling your story, practice makes *natural*. Practice your story (on and off the field) until you know it by heart, the long version, the short version, the funny version, the serious version. You may worry that this will make it sound stiff, or "canned," and at first it probably will. I don't know about you, but I find it very uncomfortable when I see someone speaking on TV, or from stage to an audience, in a robotic over-rehearsed way (often reading from cards or a teleprompter). When I first started sharing my story, my conversations tended to sound just like that—as though they were rehearsed and memorized. That's because they were! But over time, as I continued to practice and became more familiar with my own story and the details of my business, my conversations became more fluid and organic, more natural. The more you know about your story, message, and business, the more comfortable, confident, and flexible you will be when sharing it.

You may think you do not have a story, but all of us have a story by the mere fact of existing. If you sit down and really think about your own life's experiences, you will most likely think of several stories. A story does not have to be of the magnitude of *Moby Dick* or *War and Peace*; it can be a snippet or an anecdote about a particular moment in time. With practice you will get good at being able to infuse your stories into conversations that relate to what's being discussed, and in many cases will do so with humor.

Practice telling your story as often as you can. If you're worried that people won't be interested, try asking the other person to tell you his or her story first. You'll find that if you're a good listener, most people will return the favor and ask you to share your story as well.

#20

Write Your Own Rejection Letter

I don't care to belong to any club that will have me as a member.
Groucho Marx

A few of my actor friends have said, "If you like rejection, then become an actor." Actors, artists, and writers in general know all too well the ups and downs and the ins and outs of living from one rejection to another. You don't have to be an artist to understand this, but you can certainly learn from them.

My longtime friend and artist Dave Roberts has a very creative rejection slip proudly displayed on his studio wall from the famous countercultural cartoonist of the 1960s, R. Crumb, which he received back after he had submitted his art to Mr. Crumb's publication. Notice I said proudly displayed. It depicts nothing more than a simple cartoon of a thumbs down, drawn and signed by Mr. Crumb himself. Crumb created the famous comic strip "Keep on Truckin'," which became an icon of optimism during the hippie era and the Vietnam War. Toyota offered Crumb $100,000 to reproduce the imagery for a "Keep on Truckin'" advertising campaign, but he turned it down—perhaps, I like to imagine, with the same symbolic rejection slip that he sent to Dave.

"Keep on Truckin'" could not be a better metaphor for the advice I want to share here, because one of the greatest obstacles to making new connections is the fear of rejection. Fear of rejection is such a powerful emotion that it can keep you from even striking up a conversation with a stranger on a park bench. If you find yourself afraid to even extend a friendly hand for fear it will be slapped away, your fear of rejection is something you're going to need to get a handle on.

The first thing to understand is that you're not alone. According to Dr. Signe Dayhoff, speaking to *Psychology Today*, "nearly 20 million individuals at any one time suffer from some form of social anxiety. They fear being negatively evaluated in anything they do; fear being rejected; fear being abandoned."[13]

Many psychologists see the threat of rejection as being at the root of what people cite as their number one fear: the fear of public speaking. And while it may seem a little overdramatic to fear rejection more than death, researchers say that it's actually not so crazy if you look at our evolutionary history. "Failure to be a part of the social group, getting kicked out, probably spelled doom for early humans," says Glenn Croston, Ph.D., author of *The Real Story of Risk*. "Anything that threatens our status in our social group, like the threat of ostracism, feels like a very great risk to us."[14]

"As researchers have dug deeper into the roots of rejection, they've found surprising evidence that the pain of being excluded is not so different from the pain of physical injury," says Kristen Weir in the American Psychological Association's *Monitor on Psychology*.[15] "Like hunger or thirst, our need for acceptance emerged as a mechanism for survival. . . . Thanks to millions of years of natural selection, being rejected is still painful." And that's not just a metaphor. Scientists at the University of California and Purdue University have found that social rejection activates many of the same brain regions involved in physical pain.

Scientists have also found that rejection temporarily lowers our IQ. Being asked to recall a recent rejection experience and relive the experience was enough to cause some people to score significantly lower on subsequent IQ tests, tests of short-term memory, and tests of decision-making. Indeed, when we are reeling from a painful rejection, thinking clearly is just not that easy.

We also relive and re-experience social pain more vividly than we do physical pain. Try recalling an experience in which you felt significant physical pain and your brain pathways will respond, "Whatever." In other words, that memory alone won't elicit physical pain. But try reliving a painful rejection, and you will be flooded with many of the same feelings you had at the time. Our brain prioritizes rejection experiences because we are social animals.

So your fear of rejection is understandable, but it's still a difficult obstacle to overcome. One thing that can help is to remember how many famous, successful people faced numerous rejections before they were finally recognized. Check out the "Fun Facts" below for ten amazing rejection stories.

Another thing to remember is that you're likely to be your own harshest critic. The things you're afraid people will think are probably far worse than anything they might actually think (remember what we learned in #14—what other people think of you is none of your business!).

Here's an exercise you can do to take some of the sting out of your fears. Sit down and write yourself a rejection letter! Actually do it—get a blank sheet of paper or open a new document on your computer, then start with "Dear [your name]." Now, write out all the worst things you're afraid people might say or even think when you approach them and try to connect. Don't hold back! The idea is to make this letter so bad that any other rejection you receive in the future—whether in person, by letter, or in any other form—will seem mild in comparison. Give voice to all the things you're most afraid of hearing. When you're done, stick it on your wall. You might even want to frame it. And whenever you feel afraid of rejection, just think of that letter you wrote yourself and remind yourself that it can't be that bad. If you are really brave, have a few of your friends do the same, then compare your letters. You may be surprised what you learn about yourself and your friends.

FUN FACTS

10 Great Rejection Stories

1. Author Stephen King's first and most renowned book, *Carrie*, was rejected thirty times. King eventually threw the manuscript in the trash. Luckily, his wife, Tabitha, rescued it and convinced him to re-submit it. He has sold more than 350 million copies of his books and made a large contribution to the adult fear of clowns.

2. Colonel Sanders, the founder of Kentucky Fried Chicken, started pursuing his dream at age sixty-five, after receiving a Social Security check for only $105. He believed restaurant owners would love his fried chicken recipe, they would use it, sales would increase, and he'd get a percentage of the profits. So he drove around the country knocking on

doors and sleeping in his car while wearing his signature white suit. He was told NO over a thousand times! Now that's finger-lickin' good.

3.   JK Rowling's first *Harry Potter* book was rejected by twelve publishers, and only got a "Yes" after the eight-year-old daughter of a Bloomsbury editor demanded to read the rest of the book. The editor bought the book, but advised the author to get a day job because she had little chance of making money writing children's books. The series went on to set records as the fastest-selling set of books in history.

4.   Walt Disney was once fired by a news editor because he "lacked imagination" and then had his first animation company go bankrupt. Legend has it that he was turned down over 300 times before he got financing for creating Disney World.

5.   Theodor Seuss Giesel, better known as Dr. Seuss, who gave us *The Cat in the Hat* and *Green Eggs and Ham*, was rejected by twenty-seven different publishers when he submitted his first book. Today Dr. Seuss is one of the most beloved children's authors of all time.

6.   Steven Spielberg was rejected three times from the prestigious University of Southern California's film school. Instead, he went to Cal State University in Long Beach (which happens to be my alma mater), but dropped out and went on to direct some of the biggest movie blockbusters of all time. In 1994 he received an honorary degree from the same film school that rejected him.

7.   Stephanie Meyer, author of the bestselling *Twilight* series, said the inspiration for the book came from a dream. She finished it in three months without ever intending to publish it until a friend suggested she should. She wrote fifteen letters to literary agencies. Five didn't reply. Nine rejected her work. One gave her a chance. *Twilight* went on to sell seventeen million copies and spent ninety-one weeks on the *New York Times* best-seller list.

8.   The Beatles were rejected by many record labels. In one famous rejection letter, the label said "guitar groups are on the way out" and "the Beatles have no future in show business." After that the Beatles signed with EMI, brought Beatlemania to the United States, and became the best-known band in history.

9.   Authors Jack Canfield and Mark Victor Hansen got no less than 140 rejections for their *Chicken Soup for the Soul* book from publishers who told them, over and over, "Anthologies don't sell." The Chicken Soup series went on to sell more than 500 million copies worldwide.

10. As a cartoonist, one of my favorite rejection stories comes from Jim Lee, artist, writer, and co-publisher of DC Comics—one of the best-known figures in the world of comic books. Back in the mid-1980s, when he was struggling to find his place in the industry, he was rejected by all of the major publishers, including the one he now runs. He received a hilarious rejection letter from Marvel editor Eliot R. Brown, who told him, "Your work looks as if it were done by four different people," and suggested that he "resubmit when your work is consistent and you have learned to draw hands."

#21

Exude Empathy

Empathy is about finding echoes
of another person in yourself.
Mohsin Hamid

When I was growing up, my mom used to say, "Walk a mile in my moccasins." The line originated from an old poem written by Mary T. Lathrap in 1895. Aside from our Native American heritage, this particular poem spoke volumes to me, and I keep a copy of it hanging on my wall. It's a great reminder that all of us have our own experiences, perspectives, and insecurities and that we should be sensitive to the same in others.

Do you want to know the best trick for getting over your fears and insecurities about talking to strangers? Here it is: Stop thinking about your fears and insecurities! Okay, I know that sounds easier said than done, but there's actually a very simple way to get your attention off your own thoughts and feelings. You need to put your attention somewhere else, and the best place you could put it is on the thoughts and feelings of that scary stranger you're about to say hello to.

When speaking with strangers (or anyone for that matter), practice empathy. Empathy, according to Dr. Brene Brown, is very different from sympathy. Sympathy is the ability to express condolences to anothers plight. Empathy, on the other hand, is the capacity to "feel with" another person, to share or recognize emotions experienced by others. In fact, it's one of the defining characteristics of the human race—our ability to put ourselves in each other's shoes and walk around in them.

"Empathy is a vulnerable choice," Brown explains, "because in order to connect with you I have to connect with something in myself that knows that feeling"[16] However, despite the vulnerability it requires, empathy is also confidence building, because it distracts you from your own fears and insecurities. Thinking about how the other person might feel, and empathetically "feeling with" that person, is a very powerful way to get out of your own head and feel empowered when speaking to strangers.

Imagine you're approaching a man you don't know at a business networking event or just a social function. He looks like a successful, important guy. You're worried about saying the right thing, or concerned that you'll look stupid if you just walk up to him and say hello. Maybe you're even feeling insecure about how you look or worrying that you're not impressive enough for him to pay attention to. The more you give attention to these thoughts and feelings, the more you're projecting onto him a set of assumptions: He's going to judge me, he's above me, he doesn't have time for me, and so on.

Now let's try the empathy trick. Put aside your fears and worries and actually look at the guy. He's standing alone at the bar. Perhaps he doesn't know anyone here either, and he's feeling insecure about initiating conversations with strangers. He's well dressed, but if you look closer, you can see he looks tired; maybe he's under a lot of stress at work, or maybe he has a new baby at home and isn't getting much sleep. He's glancing at his watch. Is he wishing he were somewhere else? How could you make this party more interesting for him? Before you know it, you're shaking his hand and giving him some candy, your own fears forgotten.

And the good news is, even if he was judging you and looking down on you, as you feared (which would rarely be the case anyway), your empathetic attitude is likely to have disarmed him. When you show empathy toward others, it has the effect of lowering their defenses and creating a more positive response.

Try this simple exercise any time you're feeling insecure or nervous about talking to a stranger. You'll be amazed at how different you feel, and you'll be making a difference for everyone you meet.

#22

Do What's Right When No One Is Looking

To thine own self be true, and it must follow,
as the night the day, thou canst not
then be false to any man.
William Shakespeare, *Hamlet*

This is a short chapter for a very good reason, because this is neither the place nor the time to preach to you. This is, after all, a business book, albeit an unorthodox one. However, the core principle I'm about to share here is very important, especially when it comes to business and forming relationships.

Doing what's right when no one is looking should be common sense. (But then again, a lot of sense these days in not all that common—present company excluded by the mere fact that you are reading this book). What you say and do when others are not looking says a lot about who you are. It's called character. Babies and dogs (the jury is still out on cats) are very good at clueing in on someone's true character. And so are strangers. When you approach strangers, many will have their guards up and their armor on. They will be observing things about you in a way that they may not even be aware of. That is intuition. You might call intuition the illuminator of character. All people have this and are in tune with it to varying degrees.

As I mentioned in #16, many of us wear masks because we're afraid of other people seeing "the real me." Whoever you are, I encourage you to be yourself. But you'll feel better about being yourself if you know that who you are when no one is looking is someone you're proud of.

As the ever-helpful husband, I try to help out with chores around the house as much as possible. One of the items on my "honey-do" list, to help take some of the burden off Renée, is washing the dirty dishes. God knows she has enough other things on her plate—so-to-speak. With a family of four and two dogs we generate a lot of dirty dishes.

Now, there are several ways to pre-clean the dishes before they go into the dishwasher. One of which is our dog Jack. He has been known to "clean" a bowl so well prior to going into the washer that, if I were so inclined, I could save a lot of time and just put the bowl right back into the cupboard…if no one was looking and no one would know aside from myself and maybe Jack.

Of course, I don't do this. And I feel all the better for it. I don't think Jack has any particular preference though. The other thing I have noticed when doing the dishes is that when I am cleaning a dirty bowl and clean the outside of the bowl before the inside it takes longer to clean the inside. But if I clean the inside first, the outside will often get clean on its own. Character works much the same way. Think about that the next time you are looking into the mirror and putting on that special tie or that slinky blue dress before you get ready to hit the pavement.

Some of us try very hard to do the right thing when the spotlight is on us, but are less careful when we're all by ourselves. As members of the human race, we all suffer from this to one degree or another, but if you do the right thing when no one is looking, you'll have the confidence and inner peace to be yourself in situations when you feel like all eyes are on you and they're not necessarily friendly. That will, in turn, come across in a positive way to the legions of strangers that you will hopefully meet.

FUN FACTS

Have you ever felt someone you are talking to knows what you are thinking? Watch out, because Luigi the Psychic Parrot just may know what you are thinking, because he's very intuitive. Yes, Luigi is a bird and by default the other half of Dana Daniel's comedy magic act. The marquee atop the entrance of the world famous Improv Comedy Club reads: "Comedy Magician Dana Daniels and Luigi the Psychic Parrot." Long lines of patrons always wait their turn to get lost in laughter and forget their troubles for a couple of hours.

"It's a bird!" Dana yells from stage, after Luigi guesses the wrong card during a particular bit. Can Luigi really read minds or tell the future? Well, you would have to go see the show and judge for yourself (prepare to laugh too). Luigi, however, does make a great straight "bird" to Dana's hijinks with their audiences around the world. If I had to hazard a guess, the joke would be that Luigi is just a bird and he's not actually psychic. What do you expect? He's a bird! Dana and Luigi poke fun at the idea of mind-reading. Intuition, on the other hand, is something else. When you use it, you are tapping into your unconscious experiences from the past, but it goes both ways. All the more reason to do what's right when no one is looking.

PART 4

Understanding Strangers

"People are strange, when you're a stranger," sang Jim Morrison in The Doors' 1967 hit. And it's true. But there are ways you can make strangers a little less strange. While every individual is unique, there are patterns our personalities tend to follow and clues you can look for that will help you to connect in the most appropriate way for any given person. In this section, we'll be looking at some of the ways you can get better at understanding strangers from all walks of life.

Oh my soul, be prepared for the coming of the Stranger.
Be prepared for him who knows how to ask questions.
T.S. Eliot

#23

Don't Judge a Cook by His Brother

The meeting of two personalities is like the contact of two chemical substances: if there is any reaction, both are transformed.
Carl Jung

I have often been asked, "What is your elevator speech?"

An elevator speech or elevator pitch is a short, concise, powerful, and compelling summary that quickly and simply defines a person, profession, product, service, organization, or event and its value proposition. Phew, I had to take a breath after that. The point is that it should be short enough that you can memorize it and could say it in the space of a short elevator ride (hopefully without having to take a breath). Any good salesperson should have an elevator pitch. However, when asked for mine, I have to confess that I don't have one!

There's a good reason for that. I don't have one because I have several, and which one I use depends on who I am talking to.

Each person is different. People's personalities are unique and distinctive, and what works for one person might offend another. In the metaphorical sense, a brother who is a great cook does not a great cook his brother make. My brother was a great cook. Me? Not so much. He had his strengths and I have my own. In other words, one size does not fit all.

The good news, however, is that personalities do not come in infinite varieties. In fact, since the time of the ancient Greeks, philosophers and psychologists have been coming up with systems of personality types to help us categorize and better understand each other. Knowing some of these personality type patterns can be helpful when you meet strangers and are trying to anticipate how best to connect.

I'm not suggesting that you stereotype people or jump to conclusions based on superficial appearances. But if you study personality, you will find that some of these patterns are recognizable in the people you meet. Here is an example, see if you can find the clues:

A man named Alan owned an insurance agency for over twenty years. Having battled the effects of the recession for the last five of those years, his wife, Annette, told him that they should sell their business—which had afforded them a comfortable living, a roof over their heads, and private school for their kids—and get out while they still could.

Reluctantly, Alan got out his trusty calculator, the same one he had owned since college. He attacked the well-worn but robust keys and began massaging the numbers, a decimal here and another there, until finally he was done. He printed out his calculations, officially put their agency up for sale, and hoped for the best.

Soon thereafter, as Alan worked at his desk one day, a lady wearing a bright yellow sundress entered his office. "Hello," she said. "My name is Naomi. I would like to discuss buying your insurance agency."

"Sure, have a seat," he said, and they began to negotiate an agreement.

The negotiations progressed with Naomi throughout the afternoon, but they soon stalled, and without anything on paper, she left. Alan stared blankly from his desk as the door closed behind her.

Several days later, Alan and Naomi met again, only to find they had come to the same impasse. Days later, the same scenario happened yet again.

Frustrated and feeling hopeless, Alan related his experience to a friend who then suggested that Alan might benefit from learning more about personality types; perhaps that would provide some insight into where his negotiations with Naomi were getting stuck. Over the following days and weeks, Alan did just that and soon realized something remarkable.

Throughout his communications with Naomi, he had been telling her what he thought she would want to hear—zeros and ones, analytical data and statistics, and so on—because that's exactly the kind of information that he himself would have liked to hear. He had never paid attention to the signals she was giving him about what mattered to her, which would have helped him to say the things *she* wanted to hear.

When he thought back over his conversations with Naomi, he remembered the feelings she expressed about wanting to help young families who are just starting out with their insurance needs. He recalled how she had told him of her trip to the ravaged South after Hurricane Katrina and how it gave her the inspiration to own her own insurance business. He remembered the questions she had asked about his kids and *their* feelings about his business. She'd even asked if he had a dog! It all became clear; Naomi had a "nurturing" personality, whereas Alan's personality was more analytical. As a result, he had been speaking the wrong language to her and stalling the sale!

Alan quickly retooled his communications with Naomi. He changed the "conversation" from an analytical data-driven discussion about the value of the business to a nurturing discussion about the *values* of the business. Not only did he make the sale, but he also got a higher price than he even asked in the first place!

There are many different personality-type systems out there, and I encourage you to do some research and find one that resonates with you. The Greek physician Hippocrates, who was born around 460 B.C. on the island of Cos, off the southwest coast of present-day Turkey, and is considered to be the founding father of medicine as a rational science, came up with the idea of the "Four Humors."

He stated that health is a harmonious balance of four humors and that disease results from their disharmony and imbalance. The etymology (that's a fancy word for the study of the origin of words) of the word *humor* came from this fact. Ironically, it is not clear how it ended up representing something funny. The theory holds that the human body is filled with four basic substances, called *humors*, which are in balance when a person is healthy. All diseases and disabilities resulted from an excess or deficit of one of these four humors. The four humors are black bile, yellow bile, phlegm, and blood.

The four humors were the precursor to Hippocrates' theory of the four temperaments, where he suggested that all people can be categorized into one of four different personality types: Sanguine (pleasure-seeking and sociable), Choleric (ambitious and leader-like), Melancholic (analytical and quiet), and Phlegmatic (relaxed and peaceful).

Hippocrates lived a very long life and died at a ripe old age in the town of Larissa in Thessaly. His work paved the way for a plethora of modern systems of personality types. There is not one definitive system, but many of the more popular ones have some similarities. Here are a few you might be interested in checking out: the Myers-Briggs system, the Sixteen Personalities, the Interaction Styles model by Linda Berens, and the one I personally have used to great effect over the years, the B.A.N.K system, created by my friend Cheri Tree.

Some of these systems may at first seem like an over-simplification of the rich tapestry of human personality, but with a little study, the power of these perspectives will reveal itself. Einstein once said that any intelligent fool can make things bigger and more complex, but it takes a touch of genius and a lot of courage to move in the opposite direction.

Cheri Tree is one of those few who have moved in the opposite direction. Cheri has made millions in sales and has taken her vast experience and distilled the idea of the four personality types down to something so simple, easy, and applicable that it is brilliant. There are two key components that make B.A.N.K. so successful.

Tony Robbins has said, "Let your prospect determine your presentation." Many people in sales approach their prospects with what they think their prospects wants to hear based on their *own* personality rather than that of the prospects. This is the first part of the equation and what planted the seed for Cheri to create B.A.N.K.

Imagine if you could deduce a person's personality type while you were talking to them. What if you found out that they had a nurturing type of personality rather than an action-taker type? That, of course, would be very valuable information. Would you not, in turn, change your conversation or presentation to connect with that person on his or her level? Would that not also help with personal relationships too? I believe that teachers, pastors, police officers—anyone who deals with people—could benefit from this knowledge.

B.A.N.K. is an acronym for the four personality traits simplified in such a way as to make it much easier to remember and use them. For instance, my B.A.N.K. personality code is A.N.B.K. See if you can deduce your own code based on the information below.

B stands for the BLUEPRINT-driven personality types. These people like order and structure, timelines and lists—they like to have a blueprint. They are rarely late for appointments and expect others to be the same way.

A types are the ACTION takers. They like to move forward with wild abandon. They do not like to get too caught up in the details, nor do they like to read directions (this drives my wife crazy). They are usually good storytellers and performers. They tend to be flexible and spontaneous and like to have fun.

N types are the NURTURING types of people. They like to help everyone, regardless of personal cost. They are usually more empathetic and caring. They tend to want to give away their products or service.

K types are the KNOWLEDGE seekers. It has been said that data tells and stories sell. K types are the few people who you can actually do a "data dump" on and not drive them away. They tend to be more analytical and science driven and in many cases "sell themselves" on your product or service based on all of the data you give them.

Of course, none of us is just one of these types. But we are more inclined toward some and less toward others. That's why we each have a four-letter code that reflects the order of priority these four types take in our particular personalities. Look at each person you meet and know that they too have their own code just like you. Their story is as important as yours, and it will most likely be different too!

The next time you are conversing with a stranger, try to guess their personality code beforehand. As you converse with them, you'll be able to test whether your initial instinct was correct. Once you have established trust, you can even come right out and ask the person what they feel their own personality type is. Most people are curious when it comes to how their own personality comes across to others. The more you practice this kind of observation, the quicker you'll be able to read the clues and the more accurate your guesses will be.

Observe and take note of clothing, jewelry, and body language when speaking to strangers. These can be telltale signs as to which personality type they may be. For instance, if someone has a tie-dyed shirt on, chances are they are NOT a K type personality in the B.A.N.K. system. First impressions aren't always accurate, however. You need to assess a person by asking questions and listening in conjunction with visual observation, and then put all the pieces together. It's not easy to master, but with a little work you will find that your communication with others will improve.

#24

Be Unassuming

Your assumptions are your windows on the world.
Scrub them off every once in a while,
or the light won't come in.
Alan Alda

I am not one in a million; I am one of three. A third, as in "the third" Stan in my family lineage. My grandfather was also named Stan, Stan Sr., but we affectionately called him Grumps, because as he grew older he could be a bit edgy at times. He was a softie at heart, though, and he loved people and sharing stories about who he met and the places he visited.

One of Grumps's best qualities was that he was unassuming, which is a very likable trait indeed, but more importantly, one that helps open doors and creates opportunities.

In the early 1950s, Grumps, a passionate sailor, frequented the Newport Harbor Yacht Club in Newport Beach, California. There he would sit in the empty bar, alone, for hours at a time and sip his drink while making small talk with the not-so-busy bartender as they watched other sailors come and go. The window in the bar overlooked the sea and the small marina where boats would dock alongside the building. He spent many an evening there watching the sea swallow the sun.

One lazy sunny afternoon, as several boats moved like little ants across the horizon, Grumps spotted one in particular that made its way toward the dock that sat beneath the bar. As the boat got closer, its shape and size became more apparent and soon filled the window. At least sixty feet from bow to stern, it was a schooner with two giant masts. Ropes were slung and the boat was moored and secured. A dark-haired gentleman, unshaven and a little disheveled, wearing ragged khaki pants, an old greasy sweatshirt, and dark sunglasses, hopped from deck to dock and walked up the ramp to the bar. "Ahoy, gentleman," the man said as he entered the bar.

Despite his unkempt appearance, Grumps welcomed him, slapped the bar, and said, "Have a seat, good sir. I'll buy you a drink." And that he did. The minutes soon turned to hours and the sun began to set. Eventually, the man stood, slapped Grumps on the back, and said, "Thanks for the drinks, Stan. Great conversation and camaraderie." He then walked through the door and walked down the ramp.

Grumps shook his head as he laughed and said, "Of all the gin joints in all the towns in all the world…"

The unkempt stranger had turned out to be Humphrey Bogart. Most would have dismissed him based on his appearance, assuming he was a handyman or boat mechanic. But not my unassuming grandfather. Throughout the afternoon, they spoke of their mutual fondness for the sea, of *Santana* (the name of Bogart's great boat), of Lauren Bacall, and of Bogie's adventures in Hollywood. They spoke of Grumps's life and his family and his travels. Two strangers, sharing stories, became friends if only for a few hours.

Assumptions are self-imposed roadblocks! While it's important to look for clues as to a stranger's personality and circumstances, it's also important never to jump too quickly to conclusions. Be unassuming. If you assume too much, you might miss the most important things the other person has to share. And you never know who you might find yourself talking to.

#25

Look, Learn, and Listen

*If you make listening and observation your occupation
you will gain much more than you can by talk.*
Robert Baden-Powell

"Oh, look... there's a squirrel!" That's how I met my friend Ted (see #7). I suffer from the malady called shiny ball syndrome. Others may call it "squirrels in the brain." Unfocused attention. A.D.D. R.E.S.P.E.C.T, sock it to me, sock it to me.

It's a blessing and a curse. A curse in the sense that it makes it harder to stay focused on any one project or conversation at a time. A blessing in the sense that it fuels my creativity.

But as a "right-brained" creative individual, my listening skills have suffered from this affliction and are not all that stellar. My mind is constantly firing on twelve cylinders. While growing up, my Grandma Vera owned a big, shiny Jaguar XJ12 that also ran on twelve cylinders and purred like a giant asthmatic kitten. Every once in a while, I will see one of those beautiful cars drive by and will I think of this. But I digress—see how easy that can happen?

Listening is something I have to constantly work on; however, the past several years of practicing this have made me much better. For those of you who are more focused in nature, listening issues may also arise for another reason. You may be so eager to share your own story that you can often forget that others have their own stories, likes, wants, needs, and personalities to share as well. By asking questions, listening intently, observing, and not interrupting, you can deduce what "face paint" strangers may have on and gear your conversation accordingly.

When talking to strangers, you need to be flexible and spontaneous and hone your skills of observation and listening. Through the powers of observation and listening, you can be creative in determining which direction to go or knowing the right questions to ask. Of course, if you have learned and practiced your story as mentioned in #18 and #19, it will be much easier to roll with the punches in this way.

I'm sure I'm not saying anything here that you do not already know to be true. I am merely bringing it to the surface to remind you how important listening is. The trick is to be aware of this while you are conversing with people. Be in the now, or as Chevy Chase so eloquently put it in the comedy classic *Caddyshack*, "Be the ball!"

In his book *Broken Windows, Broken Business: How the Smallest Remedies Reap the Biggest Rewards*, Hollywood public rations expert Michael Levine offers that problems in business, large and small, typically stem from inattention to tiny details. Drawing on real-world examples, such as JetBlue's decision to give fliers what they really want—leather seats, personal televisions, online ticketing—to Google's customer-based strategy for breaking out of the pack of Internet search engines, Levine states that small incremental changes can have a very big positive impact. A parallel to this also applies to relationships both personal and business; it's all in the details and a little goes a long way. Listening is a simple yet powerful ingredient whether you are a big company or an individual.

Research shows that the average person listens at only about 25 percent efficiency.[17] Listening is not just hearing. Hearing just means taking in sounds, but listening requires that you pay attention to both verbal and nonverbal messages. Your ability to be a good listener depends on how well you perceive and understand these messages. Even before the conversation begins, there's a lot you could be listening and looking for.

For instance, say you are sitting at a car wash next to a gentleman who is wearing a Hawaiian shirt. You might deduce that he is on vacation, but then you think, Why would he be at a car wash? Most people do not wash rental cars (though I must admit I vacuumed a rental car one time after spilling an entire bag of sunflower seeds). Or, maybe he likes to travel. Maybe he is retired, or maybe he's self-employed and does not have a dress code that he needs to adhere to. Is he wearing long dress slacks, casual pants, or shorts to go with that shirt? Is he by himself? How old is he? Does he wear a watch? What is his body language telling you? All of these questions and observations can be a basis for guessing which direction a conversation might go were you to strike one up with him.

Many of us think we're listening when we're not really paying full attention. We may be partly listening, but we're also thinking about what we're going to say in response, preparing our rebuttals, or just thinking about what's for dinner. A roast beef sandwich sounds good right about now… oops, I just did it again. You may think this doesn't include you (as you can see, it certainly includes me), but I'm sure you've been on the other end of someone who doesn't really listen. Have you ever felt like you're talking to a brick wall, or a black hole?

Just in case other people feel this way when talking to you, there's a great technique you can use for improving your listening skills, known as "active listening." Counselors and mediators particularly like to use this technique. Basically, what you do is to let the person speaking know that you are listening to them, using a variety of techniques. One of these involves periodically re-stating or summarizing what they've said. This also helps to ensure that you actually are understanding and are on the same page.

In order to do this effectively, you need to be actually paying attention. If you're distracted by things around you or by the voices in your own head ("stop that, I'm writing!") that are coming up with your own opinions or arguments on the topic being discussed, you won't be able to do it.

If it feels awkward to repeat or paraphrase what the other person is saying out loud, you can do it in your own head, mentally repeating their words as they say them. Or you can simply acknowledge what they're saying with a nod of the head or an "uh-huh." Using your body language and sounds to acknowledge you are listening also reminds you to pay attention and not let your mind wander. And remember to make eye contact. Nothing says "disengagement" like someone who won't meet your eyes—or the holy grail of inattention, looking at your cell phone while someone is speaking!

Asking questions is also a good way to keep yourself engaged. "What happened next?" "You're kidding me. Did she really say that?" "How did that make you feel?" "How did you respond?"

Active listening is also an opportunity for empathy (see #21). Show the other person that you understand his or her feelings by reflecting them back: "That must have been terrifying!" or "You must be feeling so stressed out right now."

Practice active listening (and looking) at every opportunity you get. Then learn from it and apply it continually! Many studies have confirmed that great leaders and great salespeople are also great listeners. And in a world where so few people truly listen, your full attention is a wonderful gift to offer to a stranger. Be the ball!

#26

When in Rome, Talk to Strangers

When in Rome, live as the Romans do; when elsewhere, live as they live elsewhere.
Saint Ambrose

The comedian Ricky Gervais has a TV series called *An Idiot Abroad*. In the first episode he sends his culturally clueless friend Karl to China. Arriving in Beijing, Karl takes a rickshaw ride through a busy part of the city and tries to connect with some locals. He makes eye contact, smiles at people passing by, and says hello. No one responds. "I don't think I've ever felt this lost before," he declared.

What Karl doesn't realize is that it's just not normal in Chinese culture to talk to strangers, or even acknowledge them. They're not being rude; they just don't understand why he's approaching them that way. Chinese culture has a much stronger emphasis on "in" and "out" groups than many other cultures, and the Chinese are accustomed to only relating in a friendly manner to those within their "in" groups.

So the moral of this story is, if you go to China, leave this book at home and forget everything I've taught you! Actually, on second thought, scratch that. Maybe we should start a movement. Has anyone ever said to you, "You are one in a million"? In China there would be over a thousand just like you if you were one in a million (yes, it's true; do the math). There are a lot of strangers in China! All kidding aside, there is a broader lesson to be learned here: When you're traveling to other countries and engaging in unfamiliar cultures, take the time to do your homework. Yes, I would encourage you to talk to strangers (except perhaps in China), but first find out what's considered appropriate, what will likely be welcomed, and what might offend.

There are several smartphone apps and websites that can help you with translation, international customs, and travel guidance. When in France, you'll notice that people react very differently to your attempts to connect than they might do in London, Tokyo, or Rio de Janeiro, so when in Rome be a chameleon!

FUN FACTS

A polyglot is a person who is able to understand and use several languages. Ziad Fazah from Lebanon holds the Guinness World Record for speaking the most number of languages. Fazah is said to be able to read and speak fifty-nine languages, including Arabic, Polish, Thai, Urdu, and Norwegian. While he has proven his prowess in some tests of his abilities, he has had a few major slipups as well, including one notably disastrous appearance on a Chilean TV program, when he failed to understand beginner-level phrases in Finnish, Russian, Chinese, Persian, Hindi, and Greek, all of which he claimed to be fluent in.

#27

Practice the Care and Feeding of Celebrities

A celebrity is a person who works hard
all his life to become known, then wears
dark glasses to avoid being recognized.
Fred Allen, *Treadmill to Oblivion*

Many years ago, I was at the Renaissance Faire with my as-of-then not-yet wife, Renée, and some friends. As we were standing in line to get lunch, I overheard someone talking behind me. *I know that voice!* I thought to myself. I knew immediately that it was Olivia Newton John. I grew up listening to her music. I turned around and sure enough, it was her—somewhat disguised in a ball cap and dark sunglasses. I told Renée and our friends that Olivia Newton John was behind us. To my dismay, they didn't believe it was her!

Later in the day, I saw Olivia and her family in another line and told my friends yet again that I knew that voice and that they were wrong. Finally, Janice, one of our more outgoing friends, decided to ask. She walked across the dirt-covered street and we watched the interaction from afar. She returned and said, "You are right! That is Olivia Newton John." I smiled, feeling vindicated.

Finally, in the afternoon, as we sat in the crowded stadium to watch the jousting match while eating our giant barbequed turkey drumsticks, Olivia walked in and found the only empty seats in the stands: right next to me with her legs scrunched against mine! Having not honed my talking-to-strangers skills at that point in my life, I sat there stupefied beside my childhood crush and idol and didn't say a word.

The moral of this story is, learn how to talk to celebrities. You never know when you'll find yourself sitting next to one! Don't make the mistake I did and be unprepared.

But the story doesn't end there . . .

Jumping forward several years, I was again at the Renaissance Faire, this time with my own family in tow. I was sitting astride a hay bale while eating a giant barbequed turkey drumstick (that's a traditional delicacy at the Renaissance Faire), waiting for Renée and my kids to complete a medieval maze they were attempting, when I saw a man in a ball cap and dark sunglasses walk by with his family. (Note: celebrities often wear ball caps and dark glasses when they're out in public). He looked very familiar.

By this time I had more confidence in talking to strangers, so I tossed the remnants of my drumstick aside, walked up to him, tapped him on the shoulders and asked, "Hey. Has anyone ever told you that you look just like the actor Hugh Jackman?" He lowered his head, dipped his sunglasses, laughed, and said, "Yeah, mate" and continued walking. I stumbled back up beside him. "You are High Jackman, aren't you?" He laughed again. "Yeah, mate." He says "yeah, mate" a lot.

Renée and the kids finally squeezed through the narrow exit of the maze and rejoined me. "Guess who I just met," I said, delighted, "Hugh Jackman!" I pointed several yards down the path to where he was standing with his family. Renée, of course, said, "That's not Hugh Jackman!" Obviously, she had not learned as much from the Olivia Newton-John experience as I had.

Later that day, I was once again waiting while my family played at an attraction, this time it was making giant bubbles. I turned to the side and saw Hugh standing alone but holding his baby while he watched his kids making bubbles alongside mine. I walked over and stood beside him, silent for several minutes. Finally, without turning, I said to him out of the corner of my mouth, "Do you want to hear a funny story?" Of course, he replied, "Yeah, mate." So I gave him the complete rendition of my Olivia Newton John story and how no one I was with believed that it was her. When I was done, I told him that my wife did not believe that I had in fact met him, Hugh Jackman, and that when I pointed him out, she had said, "That's not Hugh Jackman!"

"May I bring her over and introduce you?' I asked. "Yeah, mate," he said.

I went and got Renée and hauled her over. Triumphantly, I said, "Renée I'd like you to meet Hugh Jackman." Before she could say anything, he lowered his dark glasses, looked her in the eyes, and said, "You've been wrong twice!"

We then stood there and talked with Hugh for another twenty minutes as our kids played together. Of course, my kids had no idea that their newfound friends were the children of a movie star, and they played together, uninhibited, as if they'd known each other for years.

At the time, I reflected on how much we can all learn from our kids when it comes to making friends, but I also learned something that day that I did not realize until much later. When you meet a celebrity but treat him or her as a normal person (and they really are normal people, after all), and you treat them with respect yet don't fawn over them, they respect that and it makes it much easier to "cut through the celebrity." The same applies to anyone in a position of stature. Celebrities and people in power are so used people trying to get something from them that they find it very refreshing and comforting when someone doesn't do that. To create an atmosphere of trust and reciprocity with celebrities, treat them like real people, because, after all, that's what they are.

#28

Don't Put People on Pedestals

As experience widens, one begins to see how
much upon a level all human things are.
Joseph Farrell

Vernon Bergfalk is very direct and straightforward yet unassuming, and he loves to talk to new people. When I first met Vernon, my son William and I were walking our dog Jack along a forested path. We heard a voice call out through the trees, "Hey, that's a very handsome dog you have there. Come over here and sit down for spell." Even Jack looked up as though he somehow knew the compliment was meant for him.

Over to the side of the trail sat a large and very shiny A-class RV with all of the amenities you would expect from such a fine rolling-home-on-wheels. And under the awning attached to the RV sat Vernon.

Before William, Jack, and I even reached the table where he sat, Vernon was already three sentences down the road into one of his stories. These were not the incoherent ramblings of old man but the fascinating tales of a very coherent and vibrant older gentleman who had some great life experiences to share. And he wasn't shy about doing so either.

As he patted Jack's head, he continued: "I was a sergeant in the Air Force and worked for the government during the Vietnam War era on Air Force One. The relentless hours were grueling and took their toll on my crew and myself. We could hardly wait until the weekends to get a reprieve.

"Then President Kennedy came along. He would often sneak out on the weekends to visit one of his 'friends' rather spontaneously. This meant that my team and I would have to work through the entire weekend to prepare and ready Air Force One for the flight and the return flight. It became quite a habit, which didn't sit too well with us. Finally, I had had enough. I believe in speaking my mind, so I did.

"Back then it was much easier to approach and speak to the president without the secret service jumping in immediately, especially in the capacity that I held. One day while the president was boarding Air Force One, I spoke up. This was about eight months before his tragic death in Dallas, Texas.

"I walked up and introduced myself and said, 'Mr. President, with all due respect, my crew and I work relentless hours to take care of Air Force One for you. Under the best of circumstances we do an eighty-hour workweek. But when you decide to go visit your friend, we have to work the entire weekend on top of it. We work hard and need our time off. I also like to go to church on Sundays.'"

As William, Jack (yes, Jack is a great listener too, although I'm not sure he follows politics at all), and I were drawn into his story, we could only imagine the tenseness of the moment.

"After I had said my piece and cooled down," Vernon continued, "I thought my career would be ruined, as did many of my crew. I was worried about it. But speaking my mind directly had always worked for the better for me in the past. About a week later, a call came into the hangar. They said the White House was calling. I thought that was strange because the usual protocol for Air Force One didn't normally work that way.

"I went to the phone and on the other end was the president himself, John F. Kennedy. He told me that he had thought about what I had said and asked me what he could do to make me happy. I told him, very politely, that if in the future, he could schedule a little less spontaneously on the weekends, it would be great. And he did it."

Vernon's story is a great example of how to interact with people who are powerful, rich, or famous. If he'd said nothing, putting the president on a pedestal and assuming he didn't have the right to ask, he would have done a disservice to himself, his team, and to the president as well. He wouldn't have given the president the opportunity to do the right thing—so ironically, by putting him on a pedestal, he would have made him a lesser man. By being respectful but forthright, and treating the president first and foremost like another human being who would do the right thing if given the opportunity (at least by his crew, if not by his wife), he created a better outcome for himself and his team.

Remember this when you find yourself in situations where you have a chance to interact with a celebrity or a powerful decision-maker. He or she is above all a human being, just like you, and will probably appreciate being approached that way. Of course, there will be some celebrities or power-holders who take offense or demand deference, but those are probably not the ones you want to be wasting your precious time on. Resist the temptation to put people on pedestals. It's who they are and how they behave when they're standing on the same level as you that matters.

FUN FACT

John F. Kennedy was not all that comfortable being put on a pedestal, and his political aspirations were originally not that high either. In fact, a recording he made in the early 1960s reveals that his foray into politics was a bit accidental. He describes how he was "at loose ends" at the end of the war, but was reluctant to go to law school or follow a business career. He chose politics instead because "for all the Irish immigrants, the way up in Boston was clearly charted. The doors of business were shut. The way to rise above being a laborer was through politics."[18]

#29

Be Nice to the Gatekeepers

If a man be gracious and courteous to strangers,
it shows he is a citizen of the world.
Francis Bacon

"If you weren't so worried about your ugly haircut, you probably would have gotten my food here faster." I actually overheard this one evening as I sat in a booth at a café.

Next time you are out to lunch or dinner at a restaurant, observe how the people around you treat the waiter or waitress. This is what is referred to as "The Waiter Rule," a common belief that one's true character can be revealed by how one treats staff or service workers. This rule is one of thirty-three in William H. Swanson's influential book *Unwritten Rules of Management*. He writes: "A person who is nice to you but rude to the waiter, or to others, is not a nice person, much less someone you would want to build a relationship with, business or not."[19]

Del Jones explains the thinking behind the principle in a *USA Today* article:

CEOs live in a Lake Wobegon world where every dinner or lunch partner is above average in their deference. How others treat the CEO says nothing, they say. But how others treat the waiter is like a magical window into the soul.

And beware of anyone who pulls out the power card to say something like, "I could buy this place and fire you," or "I know the owner and I could have you fired." Those who say such things have revealed more about their character than about their wealth and power.[20]

I have had the pleasure of dinning with the actor Stephen Baldwin on a few occasions. One of the things I observed is that he was very gracious to the staff as well as the autograph seekers who kept coming by our table—several wanting autographs. He set a perfect example for The Waiter Rule.

We should treat all friends, acquaintances, and strangers with equal and due respect regardless of who they are and whether they can do anything for us or not. In other words, follow the Golden Rule. In the business of sales and relationship building, I have a version of the Waiter Rule called the "Gatekeeper Rule."

It's simple: "Be nice to the gatekeepers." These are the receptionists, administration people, security officers, doormen, etc., who are on the front lines or act as the "gatekeepers" for the decision-makers that you may want to connect with or work with. And you should do this not just because they hold the keys to the gate, but because it's also the right thing to do. And you never know; they may run the company someday too.

If you keep trying to call someone and you get her executive assistant, enroll him as your ally. Explain that you've tried to reach her a few times and ask him if he could help by suggesting a better time to call. Say thank you. Let him know you appreciate what a tough job it must be to schedule such a busy person.

When you visit a business, developing a rapport with the person at the front desk will also help to establish the kind of person you are with an entire office. By doing this you can create a reputation of being fun, nice, and pleasant, which in the figurative sense will help you acquire the keys to the kingdom! (Unless you are meeting at Disney—which I have done. There they will hand you the keys to the Magic Kingdom.)

As an example, I produced several promotional giveaways specifically for the gatekeepers of the advertising agencies, PR firms, and printers that I used to call on for my design studio. (I'll talk more about creating custom gifts in #33.) These items were usually custom made and unique, such as a cafeteria tray with The LooneyBin° logo stenciled across it that the said gatekeeper could use to enjoy his or her lunch and look as though he or she belonged in the looney bin.

Another promotional item or gatekeeper gift I used was a bag of peanuts with a special label attached to the top of the bag that read: "Nutz from The LooneyBin." I would give these to the folks who worked the front desks, always leaving a bag or two behind, regardless of whether we interacted or not. After two or three visits to a particular printer I frequented, one young lady (a "gatekeeper" who happened to have hypoglycemia, or low blood sugar, I later found out) would standup, reach her arms out, and ask if I had brought her some peanuts. As I sat in the reception area, she would tear the label off, devour the peanuts, and then run into her boss's office with the label and say, "The LooneyBin is here waiting for you." I guess you could say I gave peanuts to strangers in this case.

Be nice to the gatekeepers, for you never know how many "keys" they hold. Oh yeah, and one last piece of advice: if you do choose to give a gatekeeper an editable gift, just make sure it is fresh! I learned that the hard way.

#30

Squeak Your Wheel

He who asks a question is a fool for
five minutes; he who does not ask
a question remains a fool forever.
Chinese Proverb

Eric Sanchez, a PR consultant from Washington, D.C., is a huge fan of Kenny Loggins. Loggins is known for many great hits of the 1970s and 1980s, and wrote the theme songs for the hit movies Caddyshack and Footloose among many other memorable tunes.

One day, Eric decided that he would like to have Kenny Loggins perform a private show for him. At the time, Eric didn't know Kenny; he only admired him and listened to his music. Even his friends thought he was nuts. How could he possibly make that happen?

In a moment of inspiration, Eric visited the crowdfunding website Kickstarter.com and set up an account and a page with the title "I want Kenny Loggins to play in my living room." He invited people to contribute to his campaign and offered a guaranteed seat in the "Loggins Living Room" concert to anyone who donated. Many other Loggins fans from around the country chipped in—hoping also to be a part of it—and soon the endeavor picked up some steam. Eric's efforts made it onto national television, and eventually Kenny Loggins got wind of it and called him.

Eric came right out and asked Loggins if he would perform for him. Loggins told Eric that if he raised $30,000, he would do it. Eric decided that any money raised over the goal would be donated to help breast cancer survivors and caregivers with Imerman Angels, a non-profit organization, because his mother, Yolanda, is a breast cancer survivor.

Eric posted the news that Kenny himself would meet the challenge, and it immediately went viral. The counter on his Kickstarter page ticked upward and upward, and when it reached the $29,500 mark, Loggins himself chipped in the final $500.

Eric Sanchez is now having a private Kenny Loggins concert in his living room! And while doing so, he will be a part of Loggins's next album, which will also be recorded there. But the best part is, Eric now has a new friend—who was a stranger—who is also an international rock star.

Don't assume that rich and powerful people are unapproachable. Sometimes all you need to do is just ask. Yes, they may be busy and subject to a lot of demands, but a sincere question (or a great idea) could catch their attention nonetheless.

Experience would have told Eric that it would not be possible to create such an outcome. Experience is not a bad thing; you just need to nurture and manage it and know when to ignore it and when not to. That is what is called wisdom. And remember, it never hurts to ask.

PART 5

Using Humor to
Create Connection

Humor is your friend and can open doors to conversations with strangers in ways that you may never have imagined. It can help "break the ice" and make social situations more fun and exciting. It can make your workplace atmosphere fun to be around and diffuse office arguments. It can take an uncomfortable situation and turn it from tolerable to enjoyable. In this section of the book, I'll be encouraging you to get out and have some fun!

Back in the early days of my design business, I would spend all day holed up in my studio, which my wife somewhat affectionately nicknamed the "Mole Hole." And fair enough, it was very dark, quiet, and sometimes lonely. Only the bright glow from a multitude of little orange lights could be seen along with the constant low droning sound of whirring hard drives, much like a submarine. I would often emerge from my "inner sanctum," as I liked to call it, with squinted eyes and a furrowed brow. I owe a lot to the Mole Hole, but it was not exactly conducive to creating new relationships when I began my sales career.

Then one day, I got a message on my voicemail. It sounded like a decrepit ninety-year -old man ready to leave this earth, wheezing and coughing. "Staaannn, STAN, this…this is the voice of FUN Stan. What are you doing…(cough) Stan? Why aren't you…out…having FUN, Stan? (wheeze) Stan…go out and ride your bicycle…backward through the park and then put some bubble bath in the pond, Stan. Go buy a penguin, STAN, (cough) anything… For God's sake, Stan…(big gasping final wheeze) you need remember how to have FUN!" (click).

The voice of FUN was actually my good friend J.R., and I am eternally grateful for his wonderful voicemail messages (many of which I still have saved). Every time I received one, I would smile and trudge forth as a soldier of FUN for others. And in the process, I learned how a sense of humor is invaluable to making friends, and yes, to making sales as well.

People need fun and levity in their lives. With all of the current stresses of the world that we deal with today, there is a deficit of humor in many people's lives. Many years ago, Danny Mora (whom I still stay in contact with, and who can be seen in the Kevin Costner movie McFarland, USA) hosted a comedy show that I would frequent almost every week. I got to see the likes of Kevin Nealon and Rita Rudner before most people knew who they were. I sat at the bar with Rita one night, bought her a drink, shared stories, and laughed some more. But every morning after my foray to the comedy club, I was up and at 'em, recharged and enlivened. I also learned a thing or two about comedy.

If you make just one person happy or get one laugh on any given day, you have done your job. Plenty of studies show that, during laughter, the levels of stress hormones like Cortisol and Epinephrine decrease and connective hormones like dopamine increase. That's why you'll find that people gravitate toward you if you have a good sense of humor.

Humor disarms people. As Joe Costello writes in Entrepreneur magazine, "Humor can knock a person off a certain track and open his or her mind to seeing something different. Humor produces incongruent situations."[21] This book is all about creating incongruent situations and throwing out the rulebook, and humor is one of the best tools you can use for doing this. You might think you're not that funny, or you might be hesitant to try to be funny, but the tips and ideas I'll be sharing here will ease you in just far enough so that you will see the power of a well-placed joke—and maybe even feel ready to take bigger risks for laughs.

*Never, under any circumstances, take a sleeping pill
and a laxative on the same night.*
Dave Barry

#31

Get In Your Discomfort Zone

I like to give my inhibitions a bath now and then.
Oliver Reed

Deep down inside, most of us have a secret desire to run around wildly, acting out *sillily* (that's a word I just made up) without any care of what the rest of the world thinks. I know this to be true because I have seen it myself through the work of Charlie Todd and his now infamous group called Improv Everywhere.

Improv Everywhere carries out pranks, which they refer to as "missions," in public places. The stated goal of these missions is to cause scenes of "chaos and joy." Some of the group's missions use hundreds or even thousands of performers, while other missions utilize only a handful of performers. Most of the people involved in these public displays are non-professional average people who work in unison for the common goal of the mission, which is usually pointless, other than to connect in a joyous and sometimes humorous way with their fellow human beings. The rallying for these missions usually involves a callout on social media that attracts everyone like a herd of cattle, all wanting to be a part of the fun and sometimes make a little history.

In one of their more noteworthy demonstrations, over 200 Improv Everywhere cohorts froze motionless at the very same instant in New York's Grand Central terminal, while the rest of the public watched and scratched their heads in wonder as to what was happening. The looks on the faces of passersby who were not in on the joke was worth the price of admission, which is always free. The YouTube video of this day garnered over thirty-three million views! Eyeballs on the Internet equals money. Although they started out to just have fun in a unique way, Improv Everywhere has now become a business proposition. Fun and money—what more could you ask for?

The reason Charlie Todd has been able to create such an atmosphere of silliness among so many perfect strangers—to the point that they, in turn, bring many others to his pointless parties of fun and frivolity—is that all of us have the same basic need to let out our inner child run amuck. Charlie has just tapped into that. You can too, even if you think you're not really the type for creative spontaneous acts of frivolity and fun. I'd like to invite you to step just a little outside your comfort zone and find out.

Regardless of our age, race, or status in life, all of us can connect on this level. The real question here is how close to the surface of your exterior being does *your* frivolous factor bubble? What is your level of lunacy? Are you ready to find out?

The first step in letting go and going forth in fun with others is to realize where your comfort zone is. Comfort zones are really just a figment of our imaginations. However, we all have "a zone" by default of having an imagination. To what degree can you say where your zone is? Well, it turns out there's actually a way to measure it. A guy named Marcus Taylor has created a tool for measuring your comfort zone, which you can use for free at www.whatismycomfortzone.com.

Taylor defines a comfort zone as a set of "artificial mental boundaries that determine what we believe we can and can't do." And he says that, "Every time I get out of my comfort zone it changes my outlook . . . . It enables me to become comfortable with things that used to absolutely terrify me."[22]

Using the data from the thousands of people who have used his tool, Taylor has learned some interesting things about comfort zones. For example, they can get bigger or smaller as we get older depending on how much we practice stepping outside them. And most interestingly, he found that there was a positive correlation between how much people get out of their comfort zones and how much money they earn. So if you're a hard-nosed business type (please forgive my hard-nosed description) who is suspicious of all this talk of silliness and frivolity, you might want to reconsider. It seems there's a good business case for challenging yourself to step outside your comfort zone after all.

I try to do this regularly. I consider my comfort zone to be fairly wide, but I still run up against its boundaries regularly. For example, the other evening, while on a writing retreat in my RV, I heard loud music coming through the trees. Ever vigilant and curious—and also looking for a break—I ventured out to investigate. A concert of sorts was in full swing among the other campers at the village recreation center. About 300 of them, young to old, sat around a large circular arena enjoying the music, nodding their heads, and tapping their toes to the oldies but goodies that the band was playing. Then, out of nowhere, like a swarm of locusts, a menagerie of older ladies rushed to the dance floor and began to line dance to none other than the "tush-push." They did this so fast I jumped!

Now, I need to explain something. Line dancing to me is tantamount to running around in public with my clothes off. I wouldn't do it, much less in front of over 300 people. As I a stood in the shadows and watched these women slide to the left and then to the right and strut their stuff while "pushing their tushes," I thought to myself, *Just an hour ago I was writing about doing things outside your comfort zone . . .*

What else could I do? I had boxed myself into a corner. I had to do it. No hypocrisy here. So, unlike Greg Louganis who has perfect form, I stood a few steps above and at the edge of the arena, took a deep breath, and became the unbalanced force. I jumped into the pit of gray-haired women and proceed to "push my tush." Observing my inept dancing, the ladies felt sorry for me, their motherly instincts kicked in, and I received an over-abundance of tush-push education. I won't say it was easy, but after I was done I felt great. I had survived and lived to write about it. I made some new friends. And my tush felt all the better for it!

When you step outside your comfort zone, you become vulnerable. Vulnerable is good. Use it! Do not be afraid to look foolish or to push your tush.

FUN FACT

In 1908, psychologists Robert M. Yerkes and John D. Dodson wrote that a state of relative comfort created a steady level of performance. In order to maximize performance, however, we need a state of relative anxiety—a space where our stress levels are slightly higher than normal. This space is called "Optimal Anxiety," and is just outside our comfort zone. But, too much anxiety and we're too stressed to be productive and our performance drops off sharply.

The idea of optimal anxiety is actually easy to understand. Anyone who has ever pushed themselves to get to the next level or accomplish something knows that when you really challenge yourself, you can turn up amazing results.

#32

Break the Nice

Imagination was given to man to compensate
him for what he is not; a sense of humor
to console him for what he is.
Anonymous

I am going to be a bit serious right now, because this is a serious matter and the one thing that could make all the difference when you are creating relationships. It very well may be the missing ingredient, the secret sauce, the magic bullet that will help you disarm, break the ice, and build trust in a very short amount of time. Are you ready? Humor.

Yes, that's right, humor! Do you have to be a professional comedian? No, of course not. Do you need to make people laugh to the point of falling on the floor? No to that as well—although doing so would certainly be a great story to tell. All you have to do is keep an eye out for situations or opportunities to connect with people through humor or irony (if you are wearing your irony hat today, you may have noticed I used it in the above paragraph). Small gestures are all it really takes.

In order to do this, you'll need to get over some of your fear about not being polite—I call this "breaking the nice." That doesn't mean being rude or inappropriate; it just means being provocative and unpredictable, stepping out of your comfort zone, and maybe pushing other people out of theirs at the same time.

If you're not accustomed to using humor in this way, start with simple things. Notice what catches your attention and strikes you as funny when you're out and about, and then see if you can share the joke. For example, one day while driving down the street in my neighborhood I noticed a couple workers painting lines on the black asphalt pavement. Their utility truck was parked to the side, and orange cones, tools, and stencils were strewn about. As I came to a stop at the red light, I saw that they were both just standing there, staring blankly at the crosswalk they had obviously just finished painting. I waited a spell as they continued to stand there looking at the ground. By that time, I couldn't resist. I pulled to the side of the road, got out of my car, and walked over to them.

"Do you mind if I ask you a question?" I asked. They both looked up at me with puzzled expressions, so I said, "Are you guys actually standing there and watching this paint dry? You really need to take a look at my business!" They both started laughing. I gave them each one of my "fishing cards," which evoked more laughter, and one of them actually called me several weeks later.

A couple of days later, at a gas station just down the road from the newly painted crosswalk, I was waiting in line behind several others to fill up the propane tank on my RV. Next to me was a gentleman holding a tank for his BBQ grill. He had a frustrated and very impatient look on his face as he glanced over my shoulder at the line in front of us. I noticed him tapping his foot briskly while tilting his head nervously from side to side.

So I asked, "Gas problem?" His irritated look vanished as he cracked up laughing. Turned out his name was Lee, and by the time we had gotten our gas, I'd told him about my business and we'd made a great connection. He has now been with my sales organization for over seven years, and I consider him to be a good friend.

Using humor when meeting new people does not come naturally to everyone. As a matter of fact, it may be right up there with public speaking for some people. But if your heart is in the right place and you are open to stepping out of your comfort zone, you can learn to use humor to make things happen.

A technique that I used recently is asking a stranger to help play a joke on someone I am with! In this case, my wife, Renée.

When she and I are out and we come across a stranger or a group of strangers, I will say to them as we approach, "Sorry we're late. We were stuck on the elevator." Being that we are in a one story shopping mall…

well, you get the joke. The point is, I acted as though we knew them and that we were part of their group.

Renée is not, shall we say, fond of my doing this. So the last time we were out, we were waiting in line (for a comedy show—there's some more irony for you) and Renée stepped away for a moment. I asked the guy in front of me if he would like to play a joke on my wife. He agreed, so I explained to him the above story and of Renée's dislike of this "technique." When she returned, I excused myself to go make a call. A few moments later I returned, and just as I ducked back under the velvet rope, I said to the same gentleman, "Sorry I'm late."

By the look on Renée's face, it was apparent that her fondness for my doing this had not changed. Before her look faded, the guy looked at me and without skipping a beat, said, "Did you get caught in traffic? I've been waiting for you for over an hour. I have reservations for us at seven."

After the laughs dissipated and Renée's stink-eye subsided, we made small talk and shared what we do, then exchanged business cards.

To give you some ideas on how to utilize humor with strangers, below are some examples of jokes you might use in specific situations. I find that when using humor in social situations, it works best if it is applied specifically to the circumstances, meaning it is within the context of what is happening. Although the examples below are generic in nature, they may give you some idea as to what you can say or do in certain situations to initiate conversations in a fun or humorous way. A few of these examples are absurd (see if you can tell which ones) and put here for a reason—to get you to contemplate where your own comfort zone is! And several of these happen to be designed for elevator rides, which is one of the most uncomfortable situations many of us find ourselves in with a group of strangers (or even worse, just one complete stranger).

If this: You get on an elevator and someone asks...
              "Are you going up or down?"

Answer this: *"Well, it depends on how you look at it. Yesterday I was down, but after what happened today, I'm definitely going up."*

If this: You sit down on a bus bench next to a stranger.
Say this: *"Sorry I'm late."*

If this: *You are on an elevator and someone else gets on.*

Do this: *Act as though you are going to push every button just like a kid. Or just do it.*

If this: *You are on an elevator and someone else gets on.*

Do this: *Begin to recite, "It was a dark and stormy night..." when the person looks at you with a strange look, say, "Oh...that was my elevator story."*

If this: *You are at the market and the checker asks if you would like your eggs in a separate bag.*

Say this: *"No, I'm going to throw them at cars on the way home."*

If this: *You are sitting at a bar and the waiter brings a full plate of food to the person next to you.*

Ask this: *"Are you going to finish that?"*

Do this: *Get a black briefcase, hand it to a stranger.*

Say this: *In a secret spy voice, "You know what to do."*

If this: *You are at the supermarket going up and down the aisles and you keep crossing paths with the same person.*

Say this: *"We have got to stop meeting like this."*

If this: *When at a pet store and you buy bird seed.*

Ask this: *"How long will it take for these birds to grow?"*

If this: *You are out walking and someone says your dog is cute.*

Ask this: *"Thanks, I made him myself."*

If this: *You are at the ATM.*

Do this: *When the money comes out, scream, "I Won! I Won!"*

If this:	*You are in an elevator with a lot of people.*
Say this:	*"I bet you are all wondering why I have gathered you here today."*
If this:	*Someone says, "Have a nice day."*
Say this:	*Stare at them and say, "Don't tell me what to do!"*
If this:	*The waitress repeats your order at a restaurant.*
Say this:	*"Once more with a little more PASSION."*
If this:	*You're in an elevator with others.*
Do this:	*"MARCO!" and see who replies, "POLO!"*
If this:	*Walk up to a random person.*
Say this:	*"Wow! You've changed. I still have your picture from five years ago." And hold up a picture of potato.*
If this:	*You are at a restaurant and the waitress appears as though she is having a bad day.*
Do this:	*Order melted ice with frozen water.*

Did you deduce the absurd ones? Maybe what is absurd for you isn't for someone else. Be a fool! Not in the biblical sense, but in the "stepping out of your comfort zone and doing something crazy and running amuck" sense. It is one thing to use humor to make connections, but do not go too far with it either. Always be sensitive to the situation, but always be on the lookout *for* a situation. You can't nurture a relationship unless you start one! Using humor is a great way to do that. Step out, ask questions, look, listen, create conversations, and most importantly have fun! When people see you enjoying life and having fun, most will be attracted to that.

#33

Go Full Foolocity

Stay hungry, stay foolish.
The Whole Earth Catalog

This is the point where I must insert a warning: Do not try this at home (or out in the street or wherever you may run into strangers). I'm going to tell you a story that will probably make you think, *This guy is nuts!* And I agree. I am a little crazy, and I wouldn't necessarily recommend that you try something like this, at least not until you're very comfortable with the idea of relating to strangers using a little (or a lot) of humor. However, this particular story has a happy ending, and I share it because I want to get you thinking outside the box and again really challenge you to think about your comfort zone.

When I was growing up, my Uncle Steve introduced me to the art of tomfoolery, better known as practical joking. He was rather good at it, and one of his escapades actually made it into the local newspaper. I still have an old suitcase filled with several accouterments of this underappreciated art form that he gave me—old standbys like whoopee cushions, rubber barf, imitation scat (that's a technical term for fake dog poop), chattering teeth, onion-flavored gum, and exploding pens, just to name a few. One of my more sophisticated tools of the trade is an extendable utensil that telescopes out into a regular sized fork with a three-foot handle.

While out and about at my local outdoor mall one day, I was feeling rather upbeat. As I strode down the corridor of various clothing stores, bookstores, gift shops, and department stores, stopping here and there, I walked by an eatery that is very popular with the lunch crowd.

This particular restaurant has an outdoor patio cordoned off by a short metal fence and a series of potted fichus plants that surround it. It is usually crowded with customers eagerly stuffing down their lunches before they rush back to their cubicles and offices to continue with their work while they nurse their indigestion. This day was no different, and scenes such as this bring to my mind how very grateful I am for being self-employed; hence, my jovial and upbeat mood.

Peering through the foliage, I noticed a gentleman, well into his forties, sitting alone at one of the outside tables reading a magazine and eating his lunch. I immediately noticed that his reading material was not *Time* magazine, *The Wall Street Journal, Consumer Reports, Forbes* or even *People*—it was a *Mad* magazine.

For those unaware of this fine publication, it has been the go-to humorous rag for many a boy and girl (and obviously a few adults) looking for laughter, cartoons, and satire since the early 1950s. This was my publication of choice while growing up in the 1970s. I still have a few copies lying around my studio, the covers of which are always adorned with an illustration of the fictitious mascot Alfred E. Newman, a fine young boy of about thirteen with wide ears, red hair, and a prominent gap between his teeth.

Interestingly enough, this gentleman had a striking resemblance to Alfred E. Newman. Of course, this could also be why he was reading *Mad* magazine. Either way, my powers of observation told me he knew how to laugh and have fun and that he might be receptive to my shenanigans.

Being the always-prepared sort (I was a Boy Scout too), I had one of my trusty tools of the trade with me: the telescoping fork. I pulled it from my pocket and extended the handle to the three-foot position, then reached around the plant and attempted to procure myself a French fry. After stabbing the fork at the man's plate several times, I struck potato gold.

First of all, had I done nothing more that day than wield my fork, the look on that guy's face would have been reward enough for me to pack up and go home with a fond memory of a job well done. But I didn't. After the shock of what he saw wore off, laughter ensued and then calmed. He looked at me as though I were nuts, but undeterred, I wound my way through the maze of tables and chairs and we had a very pleasant conversation about *Mad* magazine and humor in the workplace. And, of course, through this conversation a perfect opportunity arose to hand him my business card.

Let me say once again that I do not recommend, condone, or advocate such behavior, in any way, unless you have progressed to a point in your people skills that you can finesse a situation enough as to not get your nose broken or a fork stuck into your forehead. Although I am pointing this out in a humorous way, it is important to note that I have never created a situation of physical confrontation by my actions with a stranger because of the sentiment I exude to them in the first place (I've had some close calls with a few non-strangers though!).

But pranks like this one can and will go wrong. In #34, I'll tell you a story about a time when I provoked a stranger's wrath by doing nothing more than asking for the time. But usually, if your intentions are positive and your intention is to connect, people will feel where you're coming from and relax. Strangers (like dogs and babies) will always see through inauthenticity and ulterior motives. Always approach people with an honest and open heart.

FUN FACTS

April Fools' is a day for the playing of harmless pranks upon one's neighbor and is recognized everywhere. Elaborate April Fools' Day practical jokes have appeared on radio and TV stations, newspapers, websites, and have been practiced by large corporations too. In one famous prank from 1957, the British Broadcast Company (BBC) televised a fake film of Swiss farmers picking freshly grown spaghetti, in what they called the Swiss Spaghetti Harvest. The BBC was later flooded with requests to purchase spaghetti plants, forcing them to declare the film a prank on the news the next day. In Italy, France, Belgium, and the French-speaking areas of Switzerland and Canada, the April first tradition is often known as "April Fish." This includes attempting to attach a paper fish to a victim's back without being noticed. Such fish are featured prominently on many late-nineteenth- to early twentieth-century French April Fools' Day postcards.

#34

Remember, Timing Is Everything

In tragedy every moment is eternity;
in comedy, eternity is a moment.
Christopher Fry

A little levity will never hurt you. On the other hand, a big levity could do quite a bit of damage. Please take everything I've shared in this section about the power of comic communication with this caveat: humor should be used sparingly and with caution. Think of it being like spices or herbs for your conversations. If you put a pinch of chili powder in your spaghetti sauce, it will add a nice aroma and flavor, but if you add too much, you'll be choking! And yes, it happens to the best of us. By learning what not to do, you can better learn what to do!

Yes, timing is everything, and it just so happens that timing is not always one of my strong suits.

I was on the beach one day when I saw a man walking toward me, or maybe staggering is a better term (he was weighed down with a three-foot bundle of loose sticks, around which his arms could barely reach). Clutching the bundle to his chest, he slowly moved across the sand, headed, I guessed, for the site of his campfire. As he got closer, I noticed a large, elegant watch on his arm.

I couldn't resist. As he shuffled by, I asked him politely, "Excuse me, sir. Do you happen to have the time?" Yes, for a very brief instant he almost did it. But then caught himself with a lunge upward to better coral his large bundle of sticks.

Now, this is one of those stories in which it is hard to communicate the raw emotions that transpired, but I will give it a shot. He was *&^$ed! He certainly did not give me the time of day; in fact, he launched into a string of curses over the top of his bundle and staggered away. Obviously, he did not think it was very funny at all—nor did I ever find out what time it was. I have since cataloged that incident in my folder of things to learn from, and I feel bad about it to this day. I did say I was sorry, by the way. If it is *he* that is reading this, through some sort of weird fate, I would like to underscore that apology. So remember, timing is everything (and I am not referring to just asking for the time) when it comes to humor, as this cautionary tale demonstrates.

#35

Go Fishing

Rock stars get room keys, I get business cards.
Thomas Friedman

It has been said that luck comes to those who are prepared for it. Yes, I believe that is true, but I like to say luck comes to those who go out and get it—through hard work, effort, and attitude. This also includes having the right physical tools with you at all times. Benjamin Franklin, who was a master at public relations in his time, understood this concept over 200 years ago. When he journeyed about town, he always kept with him a roll of documents in the event that he would run into someone needing his services. He also did this to project the impression to other passersby that he was a busy gentleman and therefore successful. He was less than twenty years old when he did this, I might add.

Many people in sales say they do not hand out business cards; they collect them. This is sound advice. When you make a new connection, it is always a good idea to get follow-up information if possible, to ensure that the power to continue the connection is in your hands. However, I like to give people something as well. I like to leave with them what I refer to as "fishing cards."

These are small advertisements in the form, size, and shape of business cards. They usually have something fun, catchy, or intriguing on both the front and back of the card, and then a simple website address or phone number. They should be attractive, humorous, or fascinating, so that they feel more like a gift than a business transaction. I want these to be something people stick on their corkboard or their fridge rather than stuff in a pocket or drawer.

Fishing cards are also very handy when you do not have a lot of time to speak with someone you just met. A good fishing card makes an instant impression, making you memorable and different. You use these to "throw your line in the water" and you may or may not get a bite on your hook, just as in fishing. Think of fishing cards as business cards with an agenda.

As a designer and someone who loves jokes, I took the concept of fishing cards a step further when I was networking and trying to create business for my design company. I would create memorable objects I could give to people. For those of you in the conservative business sector who feel this may be too outside the norm for you, I have gotten work directly from some very large corporations with my so-called ridiculous gag gifts.

The following example may seem outlandish to you, but it was perfectly "on brand" for me—after all, I named my creative studio "The Looney Bin."

Here is one of my favorite examples, although I must warn you that this may be another story that causes you to question my sanity. But I will simply say this: if I get you to think and then act in a new and different way, I have served my purpose.

In the late 1980s and 1990s, potpourri was all the rage. A flowery, sweet-smelling assortment of oiled wood chips and other aromatic ingredients. As a matter of fact, the air quality in my own home reflected the influence of this overused odor enhancer. And it was a gag created for the benefit of my wife that would eventually become a bona fide marketing tool. I created fake cow manure and bagged it, with an elaborate label design featuring a large steer with crossed eyes and the word "PooPourri." It came in two different flavors: *Prairie Mist Sunrise* and *Barnyard Bouquet*. Now, before you judge me, I should tell you that I procured a rather large contract directly from IBM using the aforementioned as a gift, and many more from the various ad agencies I called upon. From there, I developed another flavor just for the holidays that I use for sales—*Reindeer Roundup Royale*.

Remember, though, that a business card or a promo gift is simply a tool and not the end all. When you are in a people business—and in my opinion all businesses are people businesses—the personal connection is what matters most. At the same time, if you can make someone's office smell better while you make them chuckle, that's all the better.

#36

Play Up Your Title

Titles are but nicknames, and
every nickname is a title.
Thomas Paine

If you do decide to use traditional business cards, at least consider making them a little different. A title on a business card I once saw read: "Freelance Human." I loved this! It made me want to know more about the person who gave me the card, because it immediately told me he was both thoughtful and in possession of a sense of humor. He didn't take himself too seriously, which is always a good sign to me.

The title I personally used on my own business card while running my design practice was "Exalted Ruler." I used that title not to edify myself but to poke fun at titles and to make a point that humility is more important than your title and we are all equal. Everyone I ever gave that card to would laugh. Of course, they knew I wasn't serious—after all, who would put a title like that on a card if they were serious? Humility is an important factor when building relationships and a key component to success in sales. It is what will take you from "What can you do for me?" to "What can I do for you?"

That card started many conversations that might otherwise have ended, before they began, with a card stuffed in a pocket and forgotten. Most could not wait to send an e-mail to *exaltedruler@thelooneybin.com* just so they could say they did. The exchange of business cards, for many people, is an excuse to get out of an uncomfortable conversation with a stranger by pretending they're going to follow up later. But if you make your business card funny or unique, you'll catch people off-guard and perhaps they'll decide to stay and chat right then. And one conversation in the present moment is worth ten in the imaginary future!

Think about what you could put on your business cards to open doors and provoke a few laughs or even a question or two, and maybe disarm the people you're connecting with. For example, you could put something on your business card that voices the common stereotypes about your role. If you are a salesperson, you might put "Annoying Guy Trying to Sell You Something." Or how about a card that is completely blank on both sides? A thought provoking quote or question could also be used. Of course, when you hand it to someone, they will notice that and ask about it. What a great way to start a conversation with a blank canvas, so to speak.

If you are really inspired, you can create something completely out of the box. Such as two cards I once received: one from a professional chef was an actual cheese grater, and the other from a survival trainer was made from real beef jerky.

It is important to note that you also have to be sensitive to the dynamics of your industry. For instance, if you are in medical sales, you may want to go with a more toned-down approach. This may be as simple as having a favorite quote or even a question printed on the back of your card.

The point here is that you can take the opportunity to create a "calling card" that transcends normalcy, creates discussion, and gets remembered. Be creative and have fun with your card!

PART 6

Cold Calling and
Other Atrocities

In the world of business, there is a term for talking to strangers, one that strikes fear into the hearts of even the most hardened salespeople. Cold calling. Until this point, I've been asking you to focus on creating relationships without any agenda, not trying to "close" a sale or ensure a business payback. But I hope that if you've experimented with some of my suggestions so far, you'll have discovered for yourself that when you give candy to strangers on a regular basis, you will start to see some payoffs come back to you.

Sometimes we can't avoid having an agenda. If you're in a sales-oriented role, or if you're an entrepreneur doing your own marketing, you'll inevitably find yourself in situations where you need to create relationships with strangers for the specific purpose of making a sale from the very start. In this section, I'll be showing you how you can keep alive the spirit of everything we've discussed so far in this book, while having a business agenda as well.

There is a lot of conjecture about the effectiveness of cold calling. Many sales experts think that cold calling is a waste of time. Others see it as a last resort, while still others see it as a core ingredient in the process of sales. I believe that cold calling with the intention of creating an ongoing relationship is the best route to take. Then remain persistent and nurture the relationship. I have come right out very directly and told prospective clients that, in the interest of my fees, I would rather develop an ongoing relationship of continuing work flow or ongoing sales with them than make a killing on a specific project or product. They respect that on many levels (because in that one single sentence I have communicated many factors), and I have very often gotten not only the work, but also, more importantly, a new client and customer.

Cold calling is nothing more than planting seeds with an agenda—even if that agenda is just planting seeds for the future. By being genuine and authentic you will keep many more doors open than closed. Measure your success not by your harvest but by the seeds you plant.

When I started in sales, I used to say, "I'd rather get a poke in the eye with a sharp stick than make cold calls." The thought of picking up the phone and cold-calling strangers gave me hives, as it does for many people. I just couldn't do it. I wasn't inclined to call a perfect stranger and pitch them on my art. In the past, I had never had to worry about getting work.

From the time I started out, word-of-mouth referrals about my graphic design always kept a consistent flow of projects rolling in. Some were big, some were small, but it was a very steady stream and on any given month my studio had two dozen or more projects in the works. But many good things come to an end. The recession pulled the plug on all of that and my design studio swirled the drain. I was not prepared. (If you have never read the book Who Moved My Cheese? *by Spencer Johnson, I recommend you do so. It's a great parable about dealing with change in your work and life.)*

From there, I set forth looking for new business opportunities by making cold calls to strangers. At first it was not easy—it even bordered on scary—but when I applied what I had learned while interacting with my design clients, to cold-calling strangers in my new sales position (which came about because of my relationships), great things started to happen! Now I can even say I enjoy cold calling, and I hope that by the end of this section, you will too. Or at least, I will have defrosted you a bit!

FUN FACTS

The coldest phone booth in the world is in Fairbanks, Alaska, and is made from ice. During winter, the average low temperatures in Fairbanks range from -15°F to -25°F, although it's not uncommon for temperatures of -40°F or even -50°F. The record cold temperature there, according to the National Weather Service, is -61°F. A great place to make a cold call! The average cell phone will begin to fail in temperatures ranging from -10°F to -40°F!

Pleasure in the job puts perfection in the work.
Aristotle

#37

Do Mix Pleasure with Business

The rule of my life is to make business a pleasure,
and pleasure my business.
Aaron Burr

I'm sure you've heard the old standby: "Don't mix business with plea-sure." There's a lot of wisdom to that time-tested rule, but as you've probably gathered by now, I'm not really that fond of rules. So I'm going to tell you the opposite and mix it up: DO mix *pleasure* with business, especially when you are cold calling! Although I do not advocate his behavior, I love the quote above by Aaron Burr. But, as the vice president of the United States between 1801 and 1805, he shot and killed his political rival, Alexander Hamilton, in a famous duel. I'm not sure which was the business or the pleasure in that instance, but you can't argue that he wasn't passionate about what he did for a living.

Do you love what you do? I know it's a simple question, but how you answer that question *could* be different after you read this. Not everyone is fortunate enough to enjoy or even love what they do for a living. I have had the privilege of earning my keep with what I love to do; however, if you fall on the other side of the fence, don't despair, because today, right now, you have the power to change that. Allow me to explain.

Several people, including Confucius, have been credited with saying this: "Choose a job you love, and you will never have to work a day in your life." Whoever said it, it is fine advice, but what if you are stuck in a job to nowhere right now? What if you are in sales and you don't like what you sell? What if you are stuck in your circumstances?

Chrissy Scivicque challenged this sentiment in *Forbes* magazine. "Yes, it's a wonderful goal to strive for finding work that you enjoy," she wrote. "In fact, it should be a goal for everyone. But this absurd axiom suggests that you can simply take what you already love, turn it into something for which you get paid (meaning, you have clients and bosses and deadlines and obligations…) and it won't ever feel like anything other than that thing you love." [23]

I agree with Chrissy that you can't always take something you love doing and just turn it into your job. But I do believe that you can take your current circumstances and make something new with them with your attitude. If you bring pleasure to your work, your work will be pleasurable! It's that simple. But how do you do this?

The secret ingredient to this is knowing the difference between happiness and joy and then applying that to your circumstances. Happiness is strived for through external forces, whereas joy comes from within regardless of those forces. In the spiritual context, most religions around the world strive for the latter, and there is a good reason for this.

Scientists say happiness can be measured because people can reliably and honestly report their increases and decreases in happiness levels. Joy, on the other hand, is a state of mind or, more importantly, a state of the heart. Joy cannot be taken away (bad news for any joy killers out there) and you can take it with you wherever you go.

By adding pleasure through joy to your circumstances, others will pick up on it; therefore, pleasure will beget more pleasure regardless of your circumstances. So you will be on your way to loving what you do even if you don't like your job. And the doors that will open for you through the strangers you meet by doing this will be numerous. In my personal case, that is exactly how this book came about!

Use the other tools and tips in this book to add pleasure to your work, and remember that if you're enjoying yourself and having a good time when you're building business relationships, there's a much better chance that those relationships will lead to good things.

#38

If You're Trying to Sell, Say So

I have always said that everyone is in sales. Maybe
you don't hold the title of salesperson, but if
the business you are in requires you to deal
with people, you, my friend, are in sales.
Zig Ziglar

When we are talking about "right from the start" sales relationships, the principles I have shared up to this point still apply. The key word that ties all of this together is *authenticity*.

With that being said, one of the biggest mistakes salespeople make is burying their true agenda until they get to the "close." They try to establish a connection with their prospects, reel them in, and then at the last minute, they spring the hard sell on their surprised targets. The problem with this approach is that if you're hiding your intention, you won't be authentic, and your attention will be distracted by trying to figure out when you can insert your sales pitch (or close) into the conversation.

Your prospect will be uncomfortable as well, since he or she will likely sense your hidden agenda or at least pick up on your distraction. This even applies to the mattress salesman who patiently waits in his store for new customers to come to him. In this case, even though both parties know the agenda ahead of time (to sell/buy a bed), he will still need to be direct in such a way as to not to sound insincere when he makes small talk. If he tries to hide the sales side of the conversation, by being inauthentic about that, his chances of success are diminished.

A good salesperson will find the need and bring awareness to the person who may not have realized that he or she had the need for the product in the first place. But a great sales person will be direct enough and authentic enough that the person will come to the realization on their own! Steve Jobs was a master of this philosophy, which still permeates the marketing strategy of Apple to this day.

A friend recently told my wife and me a story that is both sad and funny in hindsight, but it underscores the importance of being authentic when doing sales. The names and details here have been changed to protect the innocent. Our friend, let's call her Cleopatra (why not—we are trying to be creative here, after all), had a huge high school crush on Randy, a classmate of hers who she worked with on the student body council. Although they were friends, her feelings were not reciprocated. And, as is so often the case, after graduation they drifted apart and never spoke again.

Until ten years later when, out of the blue, Randy called Cleopatra and asked her to go to dinner. In anticipation, her old warm and fuzzy feelings for Randy came crashing back as she prepped and primped for the soon-to-be romantic evening. Amid the glimmering candlelight, the clinking of glasses, and soft murmurs from the other patrons, as though he had slapped her across the face, Randy proceeded to tell Cleopatra about a business opportunity.

Now, first of all, there should be no ill reflection on discussing business. The morale to the story is that Randy was not only indirect and inauthentic in his sales approach, but he also crushed Cleopatra's hopes yet again. And she never joined that business either.

If you're trying to sell something, say so right up front. It will also show that you are proud of the product you sell. But don't be afraid to be creative. It could be in the form a simple question. "So you're not sleeping well these days and you need a new bed?" might work for the mattress salesman, or "You have definably come to the right place. Sleeping pills are so passé. A new mattress is the way to go, and you won't have to buy so much coffee."

That way, you get it out and get it over with, and then you can focus on creating a connection, with nothing to hide and no need to maneuver or strategize. And the person you're speaking with will appreciate your honesty and authenticity, and relax—not feeling the need to defend himself or herself from your unspoken agendas.

Personally, if I was in mattress sales, I would have a dog or two running around the store for prospective customers to use when testing the mattresses. People love to curl up with their dogs! Okay, maybe you would not really want to go that far, but it illustrates the point that you can connect with your prospects in authentic and different ways even if you work on a showroom floor.

Jeff Caughren is a sales agent for Sotheby's International Realty in Orange County, California, and he knows when to be direct about sales in an indirect way. For those that are not familiar with the name Sotheby's, it is synonymous with opulence, exotic places, expensive art, rare antiques, collectibles, high-end real estate, and homes worldwide. As a purveyor of affluent living and commercial spaces, Jeff is used to the sensibilities of strangers with high tastes and standards. Sometimes they can be demanding, but in most cases they just know exactly what they want.

One such stranger owned a large apartment in a luxury high-rise in Irvine, California. The apartment was being appraised for a refinance, but the appraiser assigned to evaluate the worth of the property did so from a purely zeros-and-ones standpoint, without any thought as to the nuances and intricacies of living in the building that the apartment was located in, which also added value. Hence, the appraisal came in well below the expected number. The perceived value by the owner was, of course, much higher. The gap between the two affected his being able to refinance.

Through a referral from another realtor, Jeff was contacted to come in and save the day. And he did just that. Jeff knows how to talk to strangers in a direct way, with a subtlety and finesse that moves the conversation forward, regardless of the expected outcome. He believes that you need to connect on a personal yet direct level with your prospects within the first several minutes of meeting them. In this case, the prospect was the new appraiser. Jeff was able to show the appraiser the property in such a way as to break through the over-analytical lens appraisers tend to have by showing him the "possibilities" of living in such a fine space.

By "showing" the apartment to the appraiser from a showroom perspective and working his relationship magic, Jeff was able to have the space appraised at a much higher value. This in turn raised the value of *all* of the units in the building! The owner refinanced his property and was very happy.

So happy, as a matter of fact, that he threw Jeff a party to show his appreciation. When Jeff entered the room, he found a giant cake decorated to look like a life-size pallet of one-hundred-dollar bills in the middle of the room!

The story does not end there though. Although Jeff did not actually "sell" the property, he made a new relationship with someone who will definitely be a lifelong client. But, standing around the room when Jeff entered the party were all of the owners from over fifty of the other apartments in the building. They all wanted to meet him! Who do you think they will call when they need a realtor?

Being direct about what you are selling in a fluid and personal way will raise your chances of success, whether you are selling mattresses or million-dollar high-rise flats!

#39

Never Write Off a Wrong Number

Small opportunities are often the beginning of great enterprises.
Demosthenes

"Hi, Janet. This is Rosa. After seeing the apartment, I would really like to go ahead and move in as soon as possible. This weekend hopefully! Please call me back so I can get started."

That was a "wrong number" message that was left on my voicemail one day. Of course, being that my name is not Janet, I immediately realized it was not for me, but it also occurred to me that whoever was supposed to get the message would not. Always looking for the opportunity to pay it forward, I picked up the phone and called Rosa to let her know that her message ended up on the wrong voicemail.

While I was on the phone with Rosa, she thanked me profusely for letting her know about her mistake. She also apologized for her heavy breathing—then before my mind ran amuck, she also explained that she happened to be at the gym and she did not have a lot of time. Not wanting to interrupt her workout, I simply told her it was my pleasure and that if she cared to, she would be welcome to visit my website, which I then gave her the URL for. At this point, I was selling a nutritional supplement and using the URL EscapeYourAge.com. (It's always important to have a memorable website address for moments like this—something we'll discuss further in #42.)

I hung up the phone with a warm feeling and went about my business for the day. A week later, my phone rang and it was Rosa again, only this time she'd actually intended to dial my number. She'd visited my website and was calling to get more information. After a thirty-minute conversation, she ended up ordering more than $1000 worth of product!

This is not the only time I have had this sort of experience, so I have learned that there is no such thing as a wrong number. A connection is a connection, even if accidental, and there's no telling where it may lead.

That being said, it's important to note that in my experience with Rosa, I was not merely trying to capitalize on her mistake to make a sale and profit from the connection. My original intent was to do good and pay it forward by returning the call, even though it wasn't for me, to give Rosa the opportunity to call the right person and not risk losing her new apartment. I always keep open the option to tell someone about my website, but only if and when it feels appropriate to do so, which in this case it did.

Besides, I believed in what I was selling, so I considered it a gift. Because I was open and transparent in that initial conversation, Rosa felt comfortable enough to go ahead and visit my website. I had established trust by doing a good deed and being honest. In the end, we both benefited. Rosa avoided losing her apartment and she also discovered a new product that she really liked. I got some business, but more importantly, I felt good all day after making that call.

The moral of the story? Never write off a wrong number! Just because a connection is accidental or even mistaken doesn't mean it can't be turned into an opportunity or, at the very least, a good deed, and perhaps something that benefits everyone.

#40

Kiss More Toads

Sweet are the uses of adversity which, like the toad, ugly
and venomous, wears yet a precious jewel in his head.
William Shakespeare

They often say in sales: "Want to get more yeses? Then get more nos."

In other words, you have to kiss a lot of toads to find a prince. No, I am not referring to the majority of strangers you speak to as toads; it should be obvious by now, at this point in the book, that there is a prince in all of us. But the fact is, the more people you talk to, the better chances you will have of "revealing" that prince. A 2011 study by Baylor University's Keller Center for Research found that real estate salespeople had to make approximately 330 calls to get one appointment, and 209 calls to get a referral.[24]

Now, it's important to note that the salespeople in the study were doing the toughest kind of cold calling—using a completely unqualified list, which meant they had to deal with a high percentage of wrong or out-of-service numbers. When the study looked at the success rates among calls actually answered, things looked a little better: one out of every 59 calls answered resulted in either an appointment or referral. Still, that's a lot of toads.

I'm not necessarily recommending that you spend your days making hundreds of random cold calls to get that elusive one appointment. However, if there are areas of your business where cold calling makes sense, it's good to go into it expecting to get a lot of nos, plenty of hang-ups, and a bunch of wrong numbers as well (although you may be able to turn these to your advantage, as I demonstrated in #33). Remember, measure your success by the seeds you sow.

In #23 we discussed personality types and Cheri Tree, the creator of B.A.N.K. She asks, "Why not just get more yeses in the first place?" Combine her approach along with kissing more toads and you'll have both quality and quantity. Your yes rate will improve as you practice and get to know the different personality types, and the more you do it, as is the case with most things, the more likely you are to succeed.

Wilber You (you gotta love his name), an extremely determined entrepreneur, decided when he launched his web-development company in his parents' basement, that he was going to cold call one hundred companies a day. And he did it—every day. It was tough. "Every 'no' was discouraging, but if we got one 'yes,' it was the best day ever," he told *Forbes*.[25]

He stuck with it for three weeks, after which he had to take some time off from cold calling to do some of the work he started getting. He began with a couple of small projects, but soon the referrals started coming and he didn't have to do much cold calling anymore.

You's story is a great example of how cold calling can be very effective— as a way to get the ball rolling in a new business. If you're still relying on cold calling years down the road, you're probably doing something wrong. Notice I said "relying on"; I did not say you should ever stop. You should always keep marketing your business, and cold calling helps to keep your skills sharp and your relationships growing.

Of course, before you pick up the phone, there are things you can do to improve your ratio of princes to toads, one of the most important being preparation (see #42, Do Your Homework). But no matter how prepared you are, if you're cold calling, you also have to be prepared for some not-very-warm responses.

Some people are better at dealing with this than others; for instance, my good friend K. Ross, whom I mention in the very first sentence of this book, teaches a sales class called "I Eat Cheeri-No's for Breakfast." He obviously is very good at overcoming objections. Again, the more you do it the better you'll be.

Remember the rejection letter I suggested you write in #20? When it comes to cold calling, the worst kind of rejection can have no words at all: just the click as the phone hangs up. Be ready for that. Actually, there may be a worse sound. In the *Wall Street Journal*, wealth advisor Norb Vonnegut tells a hilarious story about a colleague of his:

A more seasoned stockbroker, who was trying to be helpful, once described how good he felt after navigating past a gnarly gatekeeper. Then everything went bad. The HNW individual answered, listened politely, and finally asked, "Do you know what I think about your kind?"

"Err, no," my friend said.

With that, the prospect held his phone inside a toilet and pulled the lever. Swirl, whoosh, click. He hung up.[26]

I would love to have that happen just for the humor factor. Keep that story in mind the next time you cold call someone and get a polite "sorry, not today," or even a simple click. Remember, it could be worse! Throw another toad on the barbie and keep on truckin'.

#41

Go People Watching

She told me she has her eye on me, so I said,
And what do you have your other eye on?
Jarod Kintz

Have you ever watched a silent movie? We tend to think that the great stars of that era, actors like Charlie Chaplin, "didn't talk"—but in fact, they were masters of another form of communication, one that you need to learn if you're going to be effective in sales and relationship building. Find some clips on YouTube and watch them. Chaplin communicates more with his body and facial expressions than most people do with words. Some of the other greats of that era were Harold Lloyd, Buster Keaton, Greta Garbo, and Rudolph Valentino, to name just a few.

In relationship building, especially with strangers, your ability to read and communicate in body language is critical. Albert Mehrabian, who conducted pioneering research on body language in the 1950s, found that the total impact of a message is about 7 percent verbal (words only), 38 percent vocal (including tone of voice, inflection, and other sounds), and 55 percent nonverbal.

When speaking with a complete stranger, always smile and maintain a warm attitude. This also applies when you are talking by phone—your body language can have a surprising impact because your energy is communicated in your speech. Smile, stay standing, and be animated when on the phone. If you're slumped behind your desk, looking at your computer screen and only half paying attention to the person on the other end of the phone, trust me, they'll feel it. I have actually made phone calls while jumping up and down on my couch (don't tell my wife that).

The best way to study the art of body language is to pay attention to people around you and see how you respond to the messages they're giving. Go people-watching. It's kind of like bird watching, but less nerdy, without the feathers, and usually doesn't require binoculars.

Go to the mall or some other public space and practice your people-watching skills. And of course, when you are interacting with someone directly, take into account their body language and your own. Another fun thing to try is to play "spot the owner" at your local dog park by attempting to guess whose dog belongs to who based on your observations of body language as the people relate to the dogs (and visa versa). There is a great deal of literature on body language, and my intention here is not to offer a comprehensive guide, but rather to encourage you to study it for yourself. When you do, here are some things you might pay attention to.

Social Distance. How close do people stand to each other in social settings? How close can you get before it starts to feel uncomfortable? This is an important aspect of body language, and one you need to be sensitive to, particularly when talking to strangers. If someone sits down quite close to you, or stands close by, they're probably feeling quite comfortable and approachable. Test their boundaries by moving a little closer and see if they move away. If they do, move back a little so as not to invade their "personal space."

How far away do you stand from another person in a social setting? This is what is known as "social distance," and it is one of the unspoken but agreed upon rules that form part of your worldview (and the worldview of anyone who shares your cultural background).

If you've ever watched the sitcom *Seinfeld*, you may remember an episode in which Julia Louis-Dreyfus's character, Elaine, brings over a new boyfriend who has a habit of standing unusually close to people when speaking to them. It made for a very funny storyline, but it's not something I'd recommend if you're trying to build trust. Most people don't like the feeling of having their personal space "invaded" by a stranger.

Everyone's boundaries vary to some degree, but there are also cultural norms that are important to be aware of (refer to #26 for more on this). In North America, acceptable social distance is approximately eighteen to twenty-four inches, nose to nose (about an arm's length). Pay attention the next time you are at a business conference or an office party; you will probably see that most Americans share this unconscious agreement.

Go to a Latin country, however, like Brazil or Italy, and you may feel as if everyone is "in your face." Acceptable social distance in these cultures tends to be much closer—maybe six to ten inches. It's important to know this when you're interacting with people from those cultures, because if you keep stepping back to create more space, you might confuse the other person. You might feel your space is being invaded, but in fact the other person is just trying to be friendly.

Smile. The great Louis Armstrong sang, "When you're smiling/the whole world smiles with you" back in 1929. It was such a popular hit that he recorded it again two more times in 1932 and 1956. The reason it was so popular—aside from Armstrong's great rendition of it—is because it's a happy song that people can relate to. Everyone likes a smile. And it's generally accepted all over the world. Smile!!

Eye Contact. Do people meet your eyes with theirs or do they avoid your gaze? Notice the difference this makes—particularly in relationship to how much you trust the other person. Notice how you feel if they are looking away, sideways, or down at the floor.

Always make eye contact when meeting strangers—it communicates openness, honesty, and directness, and tells people you have nothing to hide. They say that the eyes are the windows to the soul; make sure yours are wide open! However, this is another piece of advice that may not work so well outside American culture. In some cultures, looking someone directly in the eyes is a sign of disrespect or is taken as a challenge.

Head Movements. These can indicate many different things. Look at how people hold their heads and see if you can read their different messages. For example, a tilted head could be a sign of sympathy but could also be flirtatious. A nod indicates agreement and a shake probably means the opposite—at least in America. These things can have very different meanings in other countries, however. In India, for example, head shaking is a sign of agreement. A lowered head may indicate shyness, embarrassment, or a lack of confidence. These are just a few examples.

It's amazing how much we can communicate just by moving our heads. I encourage you to observe and study these gestures so that you can be more conscious about the signals you're giving when you meet people.

Mirroring. Sometimes you'll notice that when you are talking to someone, they'll start copying your gestures. You scratch your head, and they do the same. You cross or uncross your legs and they follow suit. This may be disconcerting, but it's actually a good sign. If someone mimics your body language, it means they are trying to establish rapport with you. People often do this subconsciously.

Arm positions. The arms are another key indicator. Crossed arms may indicate someone who is closed off or defensive. Having the arms rested open along the back of a bench or behind the neck is a laid-back, open gesture that shows the person is comfortable and at ease. Clenched fists can be a sign of anger, irritation, or nervousness.

Chris Blackmore, the author of *Everything You Need To Know About Customer Service…I Learned At Disney,* illustrates that when a cast member (Disney's term for employee) at Disneyland or any of their other parks or amusements is asked by a guest where something is, they are never to point but to do a sideways hand gesture with two fingers. Pointing with one finger could be seen as rude or too casual, whereas the two-fingered approach is a softer, gentler way of doing this. Knowing the quality of the Disney philosophy and company personally (I have created human resources designs for them), I am sure they did a lot of research on this subject and how it would also be received in other countries.

Nervous movements. If someone is feeling uncomfortable, they will often indicate it with tapping feet, shifting around, or other nervous tics. If you see this, try to put them at ease with your own communication.

These are just a few starting points for your people-watching excursion. The study of body language is an ever-fascinating activity, and if nothing else, I guarantee it will make standing in line for the bus or waiting to check out at the market much more interesting. And the more you watch other people, the more you can be conscious of your own body language, ensuring that when you're meeting strangers, you aren't unwittingly sending the wrong signals.

FUN FACTS

Body language is so important that it will often enter into the realm of competition. When professional boxers first enter the ring, they will prance and preen in such a way as to try and intimidate their opponent.

In his book *Underhanded Chess: A Hilarious Handbook of Devious Diversions and Stratagems for Winning at Chess*, Jerry Sohl states that world-famous chess champion Bobby Fischer used a very expensive swivel chair to always keep his head above his opponent and thus establish superiority. In a more elaborate display of this same strategy, Sohl tells of two gentlemen who played chess with each other every week for several months. One of the men took to sawing off a quarter inch from the bottom of the legs of his friend's chair every week— just enough that the man would not notice. By the time a couple of months had rolled by, the man's chair was a full three inches below the other!

#42

Do Your Homework

I'd rather clean a horse's stall
than do my homework.
Sara Holden, *horse lover*

Being the father of two fast-growing, eating-everything-that's-not-tied-down high-schoolers, I am always at odds with myself when asking the question "Did you do your homework?" As I have already shared, I am not a great advocate of lining up ducks in a row, and doing homework is an extension of that. But there is a time and place for homework too—especially if you happen to be a student living in my home and reading this! My general attitude is that when building relationships or doing business in general, it's better to just get out there and do it than to spend endless time preparing. However, if you're going to be cold calling in a business setting, I'll contradict myself and say that it's worth doing your homework and being prepared before you pick up the phone or knock on any doors. Here are some tips on the kind of preparation that might be appropriate.

Know your prospects. When cold calling, creating a list of the *who, what, when, where* and *how* of the people and companies that you will call on is essential! You might want to target a particular company or individual that you feel could benefit from your services. In this case, visit the company's website before you visit them. Educate yourself on their market, their product, or their service. Many sales professionals will spend more time preparing for a meeting than they will at the actual meeting.

If you're targeting a particular individual, do some research on him or her. Look for prospects who have a similar profile to those who have bought from you in the past. Use LinkedIn to find out about the person's professional history, look for common interests, and of course, check to see if you have any connections in common who might be able to make an introduction for you. Check other social media sites like Twitter and Facebook as well, in case you can find any personal info that might be helpful. (Be appropriate here—you don't want to appear to be stalking your prospects by commenting on their families or personal lives, but if you discover that you share a love of cycling or horticulture, that might be something you can insert into the conversation.)

Make notes on the person that you can easily look at when you're on the phone, including where they're based, how long they've been in their particular business, and so on. Note any of your current customers in the prospect's industry, region, job classification, or anything else that might help you to position your offering.

Write your script. Once you know whom you're going to call and what they do, focus on what you're going to say. Write a brief script that introduces who you are, what you do, and what you provide. The purpose of the script is not to communicate information about what you are offering. Instead, the purpose of the phone call is to win the right to actually sell to the prospect.

Keep in mind the telltale signs of who you are talking to. This helps to establish rapport. For instance, if you detect that the person is rushed and serious, be brief and to the point. Whereas, if you notice that he or she is casual and laid back, you might want to use a little humor. Refer to what we learned in #18 and #19 about knowing your story, as this will also help with navigating the conversation.

Anticipate objections. Objections are common to all sales situations. Objections are best overcome by being prepared and asking the right questions. The trick here is to practice handling objections until the response is automatic (see #20, Write Your Own Rejection Letter). Although you should have a script, never ever read it to someone; just know it to the point that it comes from you naturally. The most important part of handling an objection is asking for the appointment if possible.

Change your attitude. *Believe* you have value for the customer and that you're doing the person a favor by giving him or her the opportunity to meet with you. Therefore, have confidence in your ability to provide that value. Confidence not only helps you communicate more effectively, but also provides the motivation that will drive you to make cold calls in the first place.

People do not like over-motivated rah-rah either. So make sure your attitude is genuinely upbeat, not falsely upbeat. Create a slogan or saying that people can relate to that also fits your personality. For instance, I have been known to say, "I'm more excited today than I was yesterday." I only use this when it's the truth, (which is the case more often than not), but when it is, people definitely remember it.

Leave a message. There is a fine art to leaving a voice message that is compelling enough that the person will want to return the call. This is something you learn by doing over time based on your script. If you do end up leaving a message rather than setting a time for an appointment, say that you'll be calling back on a certain date and time, but would appreciate a call back. Or even close with "I will talk to you soon." But the overall philosophy of this book applies here: whether you use humor, a memorable website, or a straightforward approach, authenticity is key. That will be translated through in your message.

The gatekeeper rule, which we discussed in #29, applies here as well. Be nice, friendly, and inviting in your tone. If you get the receptionist on the line the next time you call, ask him or her if the contact is in. If not, explain that you've been trying to connect with the contact and would like to know when would be a good time to call.

Have a memorable website. I recommend to all of my sales teams that they create a website or at least a forwarding URL with an easy and memorable name. (A forwarding URL is just that—a URL or WWW you buy from any of the providers and then forward it to the company website that you represent.) If you're talking to someone who is not in a position to write down a phone number or a web address, you need to make it simple for them to recall it later. For example, when I was selling nutritional supplements, I used a website that was not only easy to remember but had a twist that made people curious: www.EscapeYourAge.com.

It's best to use a .com if you can get one, because if people are trying to remember a website, they're likely to think .com. Using a catchy URL will also depend on the stature of the company you work for. For instance, if you work for a Fortune 100 company, the name of that company most likely will have more clout than a unique URL. However, there are ways around this, such as a personal blog or "splash" page that says something about you or a virtual resume of sorts, along with cross links to your employer's website.

Doing your homework will not only make you better prepared; it will also give you more confidence to freely engage and quickly turn a cold call into a warm call and perhaps a new friendship or business relationship.

PART 7

Building Relationships Through Social Media

An elderly grandma is on her deathbed. She leans over to her grand-daughter, knowing that death must be close, and says, "I want to leave you my farm. That includes the villa, the tractor and other equipment, the farmhouse and $23,368,520.98 in cash." The granddaughter, about to become very rich, can hardly contain herself and says, "Oh, Grandma, you are so generous. I didn't even know you had a farm! Where is it?" With her last breath, Grandma whispers, "Facebook."

For those of you not familiar with Farmville, it is a game on Facebook in which you construct and run your own virtual farm from the ground up. Some say it's addictive, others a complete waste of time. Me? I use social media for other reasons, which includes business and of course building relationships. You might call it farming of a different sort.

Social media. These two words have come to encompass an ever-expanding variety of online forums for connection, each with their own unique conventions, cultures, and quirks. Unless you're a member of the millennial generation who's grown up interacting in virtual worlds, it's quite likely that you feel at least a little daunted by the idea of engaging in the world of social media.

You know it's a good thing to do, you've been to conferences where speakers rave about the power of virtual connections, and perhaps you (or your kids) have even set up accounts in your name on Facebook or Twitter. You may even feel quite comfortable interacting in these online worlds, regardless of your age, and if so, feel free to skip the next few pages. But if you're like me and many other people I know, you might appreciate some help navigating social media.

Before I go any further, let me say that I am not a social media expert, and I don't intend to offer a primer on the subject. There are many great books that will do that far better than I can. However, I have found that social media can be a great venue for applying some of the principles of Giving Candy to Strangers, *so I'll be focusing specifically on how you can use certain social media networks in this way. And since they're the ones I know and use, I'll be sticking to Facebook, LinkedIn, and Twitter. That doesn't mean these are the only ones you should use, or the best. If you're all about Instagram or Pinterest, I'm sure you'll find ways to translate my suggestions appropriately. And some of the advice in this section is applicable across any network you happen to choose.*

What I've found is that each network has its own particular strengths and is suited to specific uses. LinkedIn is not really designed for irreverent or random videos, whereas Facebook is a perfect forum for sharing these. Facebook, on the other hand, is not the best venue for seeking referrals and skill endorsements, whereas LinkedIn is designed for these things. And Twitter is not the best place to share your long rambling thoughts about anything, but it is a great place to chat directly with and follow celebrities or powerful people you might not otherwise have access to.

In the following pages, I've offered suggestions for a specific way that each of the three networks I use—Facebook, LinkedIn, and Twitter—can be used to support and enhance the principles I'm sharing in this book. You don't have to use all three, but you may find that their uses are distinct enough to make it worthwhile. The average person's social media accounts only overlap by 30 percent. Each of these sites works differently, however, and in unison they can be quite effective in creating connections over time. Especially with strangers!

You can tell a lot about a fellow's character
by his way of eating jellybeans.
Ronald Reagan

#43

Give Virtual Candy

*Social media is the most disruptive form of
communication humankind has seen since the
last disruptive form of communications, email.*
Ryan Holmes

Like most people, I have a network of friends and acquaintances that
covers the full spectrum of personalities, quirks, habits, wants, and needs.
When I am surfing the Internet, I always keep a vigilant eye out for various
videos, articles, photos, jokes, etc. that a particular friend might be interested
in. I'll share "e-candy" (not to be confused with eye-candy!) or e-gifts via
e-mail or social media. It not only sends the message to my friends that I
am thinking about them, but if it happens to be something that they alone
would enjoy—a video of a dog water skiing for a dog lover, for instance—it
also lets them know that I remember what their likes (or dislikes) are. Yes,
I know a dog on water skis probably would be enjoyed by a much wider
audience, but you get the point.

If you dare to dip your toe into the political abyss and send your neighbor
the latest scandal video, then knock yourself out. However, be cognizant of
the sensitivities of the people you send e-gifts to, especially if they are business
associates. If the folks in Nigeria who send "those e-mails" understood how
this works, they would really have something.

I utilize the strategy of sending virtual candy to my friends and business
connections, many of whom I don't know that well, as a way of building

up those relationships. It only takes a moment to click "share" and write a single sentence message to a particular person, or tag a friend I think would be especially interested in something I'm posting. These small e-gifts don't cost me any money and take very little in terms of time, but they have an outsized impact.

Next time you're online—just surfing around, reading your social media feed, or researching something specific—keep your eyes open for things you could share with particular friends. And if you find things you like but can't think of a recipient right away, save the links for future use. You never know when you'll meet the perfect person for that video of a cat wearing a shark suit riding a Roomba chasing a duckling. (Yes, that's a real thing. And in fact more than 10 million people have watched it. Google it!)

While a lot of virtual candy appears spontaneously, as I've just described, you can also go searching for something for a particular person you need to reconnect with and "soothe their sweet tooth." It's always nice to extend a hand with a gift in it, so if there's a friend you've been out of touch with, or even a connection you think could help you in your business, take the time to find something he or she will like, and send it with a "saw this and thought of you" note. Then you can follow up with the more specific reason you wanted to reconnect, but you'll have bridged the gap with that thoughtful e-gift of a video of laughing babies (if you haven't seen that one either, I suggest you do so).

The e-candy you send does not necessarily have to originate in the digital world either. For instance, on occasion while reading a magazine I will see something that I feel a friend will like. I will go the extra mile and scan it into the computer and then e-mail it to them. Or when I am out and about, I may snap a picture or two of a beautiful California sunset and send it to a business associate back East with the hopes that he won't feel I'm rubbing our gorgeous California weather in his face.

To really give virtual candy effectively, you need to know your friends well and keep up to date with their lives, interests, and quirks. (See some of the suggestions in #14, Don't Let Your Friends Grow Up to Be Strangers, for how to do this, and see #44 for specific tips on using Facebook to stay up to date with your friends.)

The better you know your friends, the more personally you can target their types of humor, their passions, or their areas of interest. You won't find yourself, as I mentioned above, sending off-color humor to your uptight colleague, or baby videos to a woman who can't have kids, or—God forbid—cat videos to a dog person.

FUN FACT

The the term sweet tooth originated around the idea that we have physiologically associated a "sweet taste" with high-energy foods which would have helped our earliest ancestors to survive. Our ability to taste "sweet" is fairly weak, while our ability to taste "bitter" is much stronger. Perception of "bitter" is thought to be an evolutionary defense mechanism to quickly identify plants that contain potentially harmful toxins. Thus, we have a low tolerance to "bitter" and a high tolerance to "sweet"'

Through their concoctions of weirdness, the novelty company Archie McPhee offers a different selection for what soothes your sweet tooth. Are you in the mood for Chicken flavored suckers? How about Foie Gras (duck liver) Bubble Gum? But newest to their line, for all of you candy lovers, is Gravy flavored candy. Their web site specifies that Gravy Candy "does not come with mashed potato candy!"

#44

Facebook It

*Facebook was not originally created to
be a company. It was built to accomplish
a social mission—to make the world
more open and connected.*
Mark Zuckerberg

Please tell me you have heard of Facebook! If you haven't, you should put this book down and go back to bed. I believe even the pope has a Facebook account. Facebook can be a *very* effective way to communicate, market, build your business or personal brand, and find new people to connect with.

When it comes to posting on Facebook, consider whether it is a good place to mix business and pleasure or not. There's a reason LinkedIn is the place people do their purely business networking. If you don't want your clients seeing the photos from your brother's bachelor party, or your boss seeing your beach pictures from that day you were "telecommuting," you might consider setting up separate Facebook accounts for business and personal. If you do use only one page, try to remember who might be reading it before you post!

However you navigate this dilemma, it's good to be aware that Facebook is primarily a personal social network. It's not really designed for doing business, and overt attempts to use it that way often trigger adverse reactions. That's not to say it can't be a very useful business tool, but I believe you have to play to its strengths and then turn those to your advantage.

I think that Facebook's personal orientation is actually what makes it a great business tool. It's a place where people feel unusually comfortable sharing their personal lives, interests, thoughts, and feelings with almost strangers, and therefore it's a great way to keep in touch with people's lives and to put pleasure into business. Said another way, Facebook is a great place to stalk your friends or colleagues.

Okay, I don't mean to sound creepy, but how else would you know that the guy you met once at a conference a year ago and were thinking of reaching out to with a business proposition has just had a new baby? If you "like" or comment on his baby pictures on Facebook, there's a much greater likelihood he'll remember who you are and open your e-mail when you send him that proposal next week.

If you're not a regular Facebook reader, you might consider setting aside a half hour once a week and just picking one or two of your friends at random to "stalk." Go and find out what's been happening in their lives, like a few of their posts, and leave at least one comment on something they've posted. But don't be a lurker—one of those people who just watches from afar and doesn't share, comment, interact, or "like" posts.

Now of course, you can't keep up with all your friends. Among adult users, the average Facebook member has 338 friends, and many have more than 1000. But if you spend even a few minutes each day glancing at your newsfeed, you'll be surprised how much you learn about the lives of your "friends." And if there's a specific friend you want to connect with, take the time to check out his or her wall, like or comment on a few recent posts, make a mental note of any key life events you should mention when you connect, and of course, see if you can find any targeted e-candy that fits with his or her interests (see #43). It could be anything, from a photo or quote to a video or joke that you can e-mail or post to friends, colleagues, and acquaintances after you have established a connection.

Speaking of e-candy, Facebook is particularly useful for implementing this strategy. First, it allows you to get a sense of the kind of things your friends like by looking at what they are posting. Second, unless they have disabled this function, you can post your e-candy gifts directly to your friends' walls, or post them on your own wall and tag your friend, which means they may be seen by many of your friends' friends too, expanding your circle. Do this with sensitivity; if it's an off-color joke that you know your friend will appreciate but his mother may not, maybe it's best shared in a private message.

Another great thing you can try on Facebook is the "Throwback Thursday" post, also known as TBT. This is an Internet "theme day" tradition that started on Instagram and spread to Facebook, where people post old photographs of themselves on Thursdays.

This is also an opportunity to be creative. A friend of mine, comedian Dana Daniels, posted a particularly funny TBT post a while back. It was a photo of him with the caption: "This photo was taken last Thursday. Boy, what I'd give to look like that again."

I like using TBT as a way to reconnect with longtime friends. I'll find an old photo of myself with a particular person, and post it with a tag and a little message remembering the day the photo was taken. Again, do this with care. Those college dorm photos might best be saved for a few laughs in private at the class reunion or over a beer; your friend may not appreciate you sharing them with the world. But nice old photos connected to happy memories are a great way to rekindle connections.

#45

Link in to LinkedIn

Active participation on LinkedIn is the best way to say,
"Look at me!" without saying "Look at me!"
Bobby Darnell

Many of the people who used to buy my design work were marketing managers who were employed by my various client companies. Unfortunately, they did not always stick around and continue to buy my work. Too often they would leave to work for other companies, and a new manager would come in with his or her own set of contractors, leaving me out in the cold. I called this the "changing of the guard."

Before cell phones and social media were so prevalent, I often had no way to keep track of these valuable connections. Now, thanks to social media, there is a way to alleviate this problem. And one of the best ways you can compensate for this issue (regardless of whether you work within the walls of the company or as an outside contractor) is to use LinkedIn, a business-oriented social networking service.

When it comes to keeping track of your business connections, LinkedIn is invaluable, and anyone you work with is likely to be happy to connect with you there, giving you a way to stay in touch even as they move from job to job. By establishing a solid contact base with the people you work with outside a particular company's communication system, it makes it much easier to maintain these relationships. LinkedIn is perfect for this, including the searching out of old contacts you have lost touch with and staying connected with your business contacts in a less direct manner than Facebook.

Just recently I found a group of contacts from a now-defunct past client of mine who had started a support group. Survivors of Blank, Incorporated (the company name is omitted here since it appeared to be a real support group) became a new access point for me to reconnect with several of the folks I used to work with.

The forum of LinkedIn is also a great way to toot your own professional horn without hurting anyone's eardrums. Think of it as a living, breathing resume. It's all business, but you can still have fun with it by being humorous or witty. Regardless of your approach, just put your best foot forward in terms of the "message" you want people to receive by viewing your page.

As of February 2015, LinkedIn had 347 million users in more than 200 countries and territories. The goal of the founders is to eventually connect the world's entire workforce—an estimated three billion people. Bring it on!

Another great thing about LinkedIn—one of its best uses, in my opinion—is that it will show you not only your own connections, but also your first-, second-, and third-degree connections as well. Search for a particular person on LinkedIn and it will show you how to connect to that person through your existing networks. This can be incredibly useful in business. And if you're wondering why it only goes three degrees out, LinkedIn founder Reid Hoffman explains:

> When it comes to meeting people who can help you profession-ally, *three degrees of separation* is what matters. Three degrees is the magic number because when you're introduced to a second- or third-degree connection, at least one person in an introduction chain personally knows the origin or target person . . . . That's how trust is preserved. If one additional degree of separation is added, a person in the middle of the chain will know neither you nor [the person you want to connect to], and thus have no stake in making sure the introduction goes smoothly. After all, why would a person bother to introduce a total stranger (even if that stranger is a friend of a friend of a friend) to another total stranger?[27]

Spend some time on LinkedIn playing around with this feature. It's a great way to make at least three degrees of separation very tangible.

You might think that going only three degrees is counter to what this book is about, but it's not. It underscores my message exactly. A stranger is only a stranger until you make them a friend, so introducing a stranger to another stranger flies in the face of that. You build the relationship *first*, then you move outward from there.

If a stranger falls in the woods and you hear him scream, is he still a stranger? Of course not! Because you would run to help—and you know the rest.

#46

Tweet Them Right

*The qualities that make Twitter seem inane and
half-baked are what makes it so powerful.*
Jonathan Zittrain, *Harvard law professor*

A tweet, a twit…a what? When Twitter first entered the arena of social networking, I personally saw no use for it. I even joked about it and kidded my friends who used it. Why in the world would I want to tell the world, "I'm out at the dry cleaners, then I'm going to the market. #errands"? Ludicrous! But soon, as I wrapped my brain around what Twitter was really doing, it became apparent that it too could be a useful and powerful tool. And it has become such for me.

Twitter has over 500 million registered users who tweet 340 million times per day. Twitter is a great way to deliver small doses of information (hopefully information of substance) quickly and without effort, especially once you have developed a large following of people that you need to communicate to.

Another great function of Twitter is that it's a place where you connect directly with celebrities and other people of influence, which also helps to build your brand. While celebrities don't tend to have publically viewable Facebook pages, they love Twitter. And while some hire PR professionals or ghostwriters (ghost-tweeters?) to post for them, a surprising number actually do post their own tweets. And some will even respond to direct @messages.

When I say celebrities, I don't just mean Lady Gaga or Justin Bieber. I mean any influencer in a particular field who might otherwise be difficult to have a direct conversation with. These can be people you look up to and respect in terms of their business prowess or their stature within their industry. For example, I follow Richard Branson and Steve Martin among others and look forward to what they have to say from day to day. On Twitter there are no gatekeepers, and all you have to do is search to find the person's Twitter "handle" (and verify it's the real person, not a fake account someone has set up in their name). A quick search will let you know if the person is a Twitter user, and you can look for "verified" accounts, usually signified with a blue star with a check mark symbol.

If you want to build a connection with someone on Twitter, the best thing you can do is to first follow them and then start sharing their content by "retweeting" some of their posts. Add your own thoughtful comments that show why you value their content. You will also notice that the more people you follow, the more followers you will have. It's a great way to soar with the eagle even if you haven't completely grown into your wings. Check their feed and notice whether they seem to respond to @messages that include their Twitter handles. If so, you might be able to actually have a conversation that way. And if you're lucky, eventually they might even follow you back.

Overtime, Twitter is a great way to build a large "community" or a "following" simply by following others and so. If you Tweet them right they will do the same to you!

PART 8

Leveraging Your Relationships

As relationships evolve through the "getting to know you" stage, they can soon transcend into the "how can I help you?" stage. This can happen in a matter of weeks or a matter of minutes. The most powerful way to leverage your relationships—which simply means to make them more powerful—is to give to people, openly, in a spirit of generosity without expecting anything in return. By doing so, over time you will find that the benefits come back to you in surprising ways. Some people call this "the law of reciprocity"—the idea that when you freely give of yourself to others around you, the universe will reward you ten times over. But the trick is, you have to do it freely, without expectation of the reward. Oftentimes, the reward won't look anything like what you were expecting anyway. But trust me, it will be better.

No road is long with good company.
Turkish Proverb

#47

Become a Matchmaker

If I weren't a matchmaker, I'd be a chef.
Patti Stanger

A match is a tool for starting a fire. Typically, matches are made from small wooden sticks or stiff paper. One end is coated with... wait a minute, wrong kind of match!

When your network begins to grow, you'll soon find yourself in an unusual position: that of matchmaker, as in matching people up with other people. I'm not necessarily talking about setting up your friends on blind dates (although you might do that too); I'm talking about connecting the dots and creating mutually beneficial relationships between people you know. Business matchmaking can be just as beneficial (hopefully?) as romantic matchmaking.

Networking is one of the most valuable business skills a person can develop. And one of the best ways to improve your network is to introduce people to each other. Think creatively about how you might do that. For instance, you may have a friend in Colorado who is a professional jazz musician who just recorded a new CD (actually, I do) and another friend who is a writer for a lifestyle magazine. Make the introduction! Or you might have a friend who just started a new business, and another friend who is a semi-retired veteran of the same industry and has some time on his hands. Ask the veteran friend if he's interested in being a mentor and then make the connection.

Entrepreneur and marketer Seth Godin explains the power of matchmaking in a great blog post entitled "'Connect to' vs. 'Connect.'" He makes a distinction between "vertical connection," or "connecting to," which is what an organization does with its customers or constituents, and "horizontal connection," or "connecting," which is what you do when you connect your customers or constituents to each other. The latter, he explains, "is what makes a tribe. People caring about people. Side by side, multiplying exponentially." And he observes that, "Organizations are afraid of connecting. They are afraid of losing control, of handing over power, of walking into a territory where they don't always get to decide what's going to happen next. When your customers like each other more than they like you, things can become challenging. Of course, connecting is where the real emotions and change and impact happen."[28]

Don't let your fear of losing control over your network get in the way of what could happen when you start to connect the dots. Trust me, it's a risk worth taking! When I would introduce my design clients to one another, many people would say, "That's crazy. You don't want your clients sharing notes about you!" But I consistently found that when I did this, projects and opportunities materialized that would not have otherwise happened—and guess who they called for design help?

Adam Rifkin is a very successful entrepreneur who is also known as a superstar relationship builder. In 2011, *Fortune* magazine called him "the best networker in Silicon Valley." He has been making up to three introductions every day for the last ten years. He claims to have made more than 10,000 introductions, which have led to two marriages, hundreds of jobs, dozens of company fundings, and many new business partnerships. And by the way, he claims to be a natural introvert. If that doesn't give some of you who are quiet and shy a boost, I'm not sure what will.

Adam's advice on networking in general is music to my ears:

It is better to give than to receive. Look for opportunities to do something for the other person, such as sharing knowledge or offering an introduction to someone that person might not know but would be interested in knowing. Do not be transactional about networking. Do not offer something because you want something in return. Instead, show a genuine interest in something you and the other person have in common.[29]

An introduction is one of the greatest gifts you can give. Think of every introduction as a piece of candy you get to offer to two of your friends! As Rifkin says, "In just a few minutes, you can have a dramatic impact on the lives of two people and generate a large amount of goodwill for yourself and the overall community you're building."[30]

I try to make at least one introduction every week. This also helps me to stay current on what is going on in the lives of my friends and acquaintances. By visualizing the dots and connecting them by making introductions a few times, you will find that other connections—ones that you did not expect—will come about.

A good matchmaker is not something you can just become overnight. To make successful connections, you need to invest time in really knowing the people in your own network. That way you're not just making random, superficial connections that will fizzle out, but thoughtful connections based on shared values and interests that are likely to last. And you're building your own reputation in the process. Rifkin also reminds people to follow up on introductions they make, to see if they were useful. That way you can improve your matchmaking skills.

When you introduce people, you are sending a message to both parties that you are thinking of them, you like them, and you vouch for them. In making an introduction, whether by e-mail or in person, take the time to say a couple of sentences about each person, describing why you like and respect them, and then explain why you hope they would enjoy connecting and find it mutually beneficial. The word for this is "edify."

They will remember you in the future when they actually need your services and will most likely tell others about the introduction you made. It's not only fun; it's also a rewarding way of giving back. And, as Rifkin notes, you will benefit too. "Humans have a tendency to want to reciprocate, so the more you show you're looking out for someone, the more likely that person will begin to keep you in mind as well."[31]

One of the best matchmakers I know is Lance Perkins. Lance knows people. As in, he *knows* people, a lot of people. Not the kind of people who break knees with baseball bats in dark alleys, but a lot of celebrities, high-profile individuals, and leaders of industry. He has been a part of many elite functions with people such as Michelle Obama, has hung out with Richard Branson, and is writing a book with Fred Schneider of the B-52s. You wouldn't know it when you first meet Lance, as he is quiet, humble, and unassuming—all of which are good qualities for making friends with celebrities.

One of Lance's many friends is Cherie Curry (who he met through Annabella Lwin from the rock group Bow Wow Wow). Cherie is best known for her antics onstage as the lead singer for the now-legendary 1970s all-female teenage rock band, The Runaways, which also included Lita Ford, Sandy West, Jackie Fox, and, of course, Joan Jett. The Runaways broke up in April 1979. Their early success took its toll on the dynamics of the band, including the longstanding relationship between Cherie and the band's manager, Kim Fowley.

Kim was a success in his own right, having written and produced songs for KISS, Helen Reddy, Alice Cooper, Leon Russell, and Kris Kristofferson. The stress was too much, and with a big falling out, Cheri parted ways with the band and with Kim, and they would not speak again for over twenty years. Joan Jett went on to pursue a hugely successful solo career with such hits as "I Love Rock 'n' Roll" and "Crimson and Clover," and was inducted into the Rock and Roll Hall of Fame.

Jumping forward two decades, it so happened that Lance was aware of a party that Kim Fowley would be attending. Acting as matchmaker, he asked Cherie if she would like to go, not letting on that Kim would be there. After the shock wore off from their "chance" meeting, Cherie and Kim rekindled their friendship and even began to discuss the idea of writing a memoir. That was the seed that grew into the movie about Joan Jett and the band, aptly named *The Runaways*, starring Kristen Stewart and Dakota Fanning. Lance soon became friends with Joan Jett because of this.

I asked Lance, "How is it that you were able to be the glue to make this happen, and for that matter, how do you connect at such a personal level with so many famous people?" His answer was very short but did not surprise me: "I treat everyone the same."

#48

Create Win-Wins

I like to think of sales as the ability to gracefully persuade, not manipulate, a person or persons into a win-win situation.
Bo Bennett

Stephen Covey, in his bestselling book *Seven Habits of Highly Effective People*, identified "win-win thinking" as one of the seven traits that distinguish the unusual individuals he observed. He explains that, "Most of us learn to base our self-worth on comparisons and competition. We think about succeeding in terms of someone else failing—that is, if I win, you lose; or if you win, I lose. Life becomes a zero-sum game. There is only so much pie to go around, and if you get a big piece, there is less for me; it's not fair, and I'm going to make sure you don't get anymore."

Sound familiar? Much of the business world seems to operate on these assumptions. We see the marketplace as being kind of like the jungle, where you'd better "eat or be eaten" and "survival of the fittest" is the law of the land.

However, the most effective people, Covey says, don't think like this. They think in terms of cooperation and mutual benefit. "Win-win sees life as a cooperative arena, not a competitive one," he explains. "Win-win is a frame of mind and heart that constantly seeks mutual benefit in all human interactions. Win-win means agreements or solutions are mutually beneficial and satisfying. We both get to eat the pie, and it tastes pretty darn good!"[32] And boy do I love pie.

I have found this observation to be true ever since I started out in business. When I was a designer, I would go out of my way to connect with my "competition," other designers. I would even offer to coach them and even "give away my secrets." Some people would have thought this was crazy. But guess who those other designers called to work with their clients and fill in for them when they went on vacation?

I would encourage you to pay attention, and any time you catch yourself thinking in "win-lose" terms, see if you can turn it around and create a "win-win." It might be as simple as giving some candy to a stranger when you're feeling anxious or depressed. The stranger gets an unexpected gift, and trust me, you'll get to feel better—that's a win-win.

Or you could do what I did and make a point of connecting with people you think of as competitors. They could be complete strangers too. Wouldn't that be a whole new market? Doing things like this not only creates unexpected opportunities, but it also starts to rewire your brain. For most of us, "win-lose" competitive thinking has been drummed into us since childhood, so it takes a little while to train ourselves to stop living like we were in the jungle.

If you happen to actually live in a jungle, then at least be like Tarzan the noble savage. He knew what it really meant to help others and not worry about getting what was his. Actually, even the jungle is not such a competitive place as it might seem. Scientists these days are acknowledging that cooperation is a powerful a force in the evolution of the natural world, and can be seen all the way up and down the food chain. Gorillas live more cordially than many humans do. So maybe it's time to toss out that old win-lose mentality for good, and get out there in the jungle and create some reciprocity!

#49

Practice Random Acts of Sales

No act of kindness, no matter how small, is ever wasted.
Aesop

Think of yourself before others.

What the… Did he really just say that? Yes, I did—to make the point that, although most of us would agree this statement is not the way we should be doing things, how many of us actually put the opposite into practice on a regular basis, especially when it comes to sales?

One of the reasons I like to spread my wings, go out, strike up conversations, and make new connections with strangers is that I never know *who* I might meet. Something I learned about myself when I dove into the sales arena is that I love people. But what exactly does that mean? I love to talk to people. I love to serve people. I love to be around people. I like dogs, I like horses, I like fish; if you are a fellow animal lover, I draw this parallel to underscore my point and to help you understand it.

I find it very interesting, and a little sad, that when I am at the market and wait to hold the door open for someone, I will, on occasion, get a weird look as though I have done something strange. Maybe it's because we live in a forever-growing me-me society and if you step outside that consensus and show love or consideration towards another, you stand out. Chivalry is not dead in our society, but it most certainly is in a coma. Let's wake it up!

Love is not a feeling; love is an action! Change your actions and you will change your feelings. Change your feelings and you can change other people's lives. This also applies to relating to strangers and business. When I talk about love here, I am referring to the love of your fellow human being, not the romantic kind, although the same philosophy applies to that as well.

While the core point of this entire book is help you let go of the outcome, the fact is if you are in sales, at some point there needs to be an outcome. Practice random acts of kindness and you will find that you are also potentially practicing random acts of sales. "Pay it forward," as they say, and you can be sure that at some point the universe will pay you back. If you do this on a continuous basis, your pay-it-forward account will be full and the flow of great things will be more constant, which of course will affect your outcome quicker.

A great example of the pay-it-forward philosophy is the Smile Cards movement. The idea is that you do something anonymously for a stranger— pay for the breakfast of the person next to you, or pay the toll for the driver behind you when crossing a bridge, for example—and then you leave a Smile Card. These small business-card-sized mementos have a smiling face and the words: "SMILE. You've just been tagged. Experiments in anonymous kindness is the name of the game. And now—you're it!"

The idea is that the person who received the card, and benefits from the act of kindness, will then pass it on by doing something for someone else. Kindspring, the makers of Smile Cards, claim to have shipped more than a million cards to people in more than ninety countries.

Visit Kindspring.org to read inspiring stories of people following this philosophy. And look for ways that you can pay it forward today. You never know what will come back!

Here's an old story that captures why this kind of attitude is not only good for the people you help; it's also good for business. Notice, I said "attitude." You may ask yourself, *If I practice a random act of kindness for a total stranger (or even someone I know) and do it anonymously, how do I get credit in terms of my business?* Because, by giving, that action will improve your *own* attitude and that will reflect on your business. That's the whole point. Quit trying to do it backward!

A woman came out of her house one day and saw three strangers in her front yard—old men with long white beards. She greeted them: "I don't think I know you, but you must be hungry. Please come in and have something to eat."

One of the men thanked her, but declined. "We do not go into a house together," he said. "Why?" she inquired. The old man pointed to the first of his friends. "His name is Wealth," and the second, "He is Success." He smiled at the woman. "I am Love. Please go into the house and discuss with your husband which one of us you want in your home."

The woman went in and told her husband about their unexpected visitors. "How nice!" he declared. "Let us invite Wealth. Let him come and fill our home with abundance!"

She was not so sure. "Dear, why don't we invite Success?"

Their daughter was listening to the conversation, and she had a different idea. "Would it not be better to invite Love? Our home will then be filled with love!"

Her parents realized the wisdom of their young daughter's words, and so the woman went out to invite Love to join them for dinner. To her surprise, the other two men followed him. Confused, she asked Wealth and Success, "I only invited Love. Why are you coming in?"

They replied, "If you had invited Wealth or Success, the other two of us would have stayed outside, but since you invited Love, wherever he goes, we go with him. Wherever there is Love, there are also Wealth and Success!"

#50

Be an Opportunity Maker

*In the long history of humankind
(and animal kind, too) those who learned
to collaborate and improvise most
effectively have prevailed.*
Charles Darwin

I recently came across a wonderful TED talk by writer Kare Anderson entitled "Be an Opportunity Maker" (if you are not familiar with TED. com, I suggest you check it out). In it, Anderson shares how she noticed certain people operating with what she called "a mutuality mindset." This means that, "In each situation, they found a way to talk about *us* and create that 'us' idea."

Anderson dubs such people "opportunity-makers," because they are constantly seeking ways to create opportunities for collaboration and mutual benefit.

I love this idea. It's another way of giving candy to strangers by creating possibilities that didn't exist before, and by inviting people to step into those possibilities with you. Think about how you feel when a new opportunity arises, when you suddenly discover something is possible that you'd never considered before. It's like Christmas morning! That's a gift you can give to others on a regular basis when you start seeing yourself as an opportunity-maker.

One of Anderson's keys to becoming an opportunity-maker is an important piece of advice. She says that opportunity-makers know and build on their own strengths, and then they are "actively seeking situations with people unlike them, and they're building relationships, and because they do that, they have trusted relationships where they can bring the right team in and recruit them to solve a problem better and faster and seize more opportunities."

Many of us are accustomed to doing the exact opposite—we seek out people who are like us and situations in which we feel comfortable. Especially when we're doing something that already feels risky—like talking to strangers—it's tempting to make it a little more safe by choosing someone who looks familiar or relatable. However, as Anderson says, this is not the best way to create opportunity. So I'd encourage you to take her advice and practice connecting with people who are really different than you. Pick the person in the room who seems the farthest outside your comfort zone, and talk to him or her. Seek out connections with people whose strengths are different from yours, because that's where there is the highest potential for collaboration.

"There's no greater opportunity or call for action for us now than to become opportunity-makers who use best talents together more often for the greater good and accomplish things we couldn't have done on our own," Anderson says.[32]

What I find most meaningful about what Anderson illustrates is that the idea of "us" is better than you and me by ourselves.

Over 2,300 years ago Aristotle said, "The whole is greater than the sum of its parts." Several years ago I experienced this idea in action from a creative standpoint, which became one of the seeds for this book. My good friend Franco Pepe was teaching a class called "The Artist's Way," designed by Julia Cameron (director James Cameron's wife at the time) to help people get in touch with their creative selves. The class followed her book of the same title, which I highly recommend if you would like to break through your creative roadblocks.

After the ten-week class was over and we had our creative juices flowing, Franco adopted the idea of "co-creation." He was soon doing seminars in which you would create a painting with a partner. In other words, both people would attack the canvas simultaneously. And in some cases it was with a total stranger! What I found intriguing about this approach is that the paintings took on a completely different energy and, when complete, were very often better than what we would have created by ourselves. In the case of a married couple painting, relational roadblocks were often crumbled as well.

And that takes us full circle. Since then, I have incorporated this philosophy into everything I do and know that every idea, no matter how private, is really a collaboration of energy, people, places, and other ideas. Think about that and apply this mind-set when you are building relationships, and those relationships will become exponential in their power and value.

#51

Make Someone's Day

No-one is useless in this world who
lightens the burden for someone else.
Charles Dickens

Remember my advice about putting a funny or unusual title on your business cards (see #34)? Well, here's a great example of a guy who's done just that, using a title that captures the heart of the philosophy I've been sharing in this book.

David Wagner is a hairdresser by trade, but his business cards say "Daymaker." He's a great believer in the power of small acts of kindness. "It only takes a moment to make someone's day," he writes in his book *Life as a Daymaker*, "and sometimes those moments even change lives, as I discovered a few years ago."

Wagner tells a moving story of how his philosophy came about. One of his regular clients came in to have her hair styled earlier in the month than usual. Thinking she must have an important social engagement, he inquired about her plans, but she said she just wanted to look and feel good that day. He decided to give her special attention, and massaged her scalp and joked with her as he worked on her hair. She seemed happier when she left and hugged him goodbye.

What he didn't realize was that the reason his client had wanted to get her hair styled was to look good for her funeral. You see, she had been planning to commit suicide that day. But she wrote him a note telling him that the way he'd taken care of her had given her new hope and she'd changed her mind. I'll bet she keeps going back to him to get her hair done too!

"I was stunned," Wagner writes. "I was glad to have made such a difference, yet the experience left me with an enormous sense of responsibility. What if I had been upset, distracted, or hurried when she came to see me?"[33] He resolved to live his life from then on as if everyone he met could be that woman, giving people his full attention and care even if just for a moment. That's why he calls himself a "daymaker."

When I heard Wagner's story, I thought of that stranger who came up to me after my talk (see #18) and told me he'd been contemplating suicide but was now feeling new hope. I felt a similar sense of responsibility to what Wagner described. In my case, what made that man's day was my authenticity and vulnerability in sharing my own story. If I hadn't done that, where would he have been that night? We all touch each other's lives every day in countless small ways, and we may never know the impact of our smallest choices. So let's embrace our responsibility to be the most caring, authentic, available people we can be.

What can you do to make someone's day—today, tomorrow, and every day after? Who can you be so that your presence might change someone's life? It might not take much from you, but it could make a bigger difference than you can possibly imagine.

#52

Make a New Friend

*We make a living by what we get, but
we make a life by what we give.*
Norman MacEwan

"I heard a loud popping sound. Very loud. And then, an earth-shaking explosion. My cruiser rocked violently from side to side and my hard-trained instincts and training kicked in. I slammed my foot on the brake, peeled a fast U-turn, and sped toward the sound with my lights and siren blaring."

The man speaking had been a stranger to me just a few minutes ago, but now I was captivated by his story. I pulled my chair up closer to the restaurant table and leaned in.

"There was a large plume of smoke and dust billowing down the road, and the shape of a factory loomed ahead. It was a fertilizer plant, now on fire, and filled to the brim with chemicals. Fifty-five-gallon drums continued to explode like napalm popcorn, spewing forth fumes and God only knows what else. I skidded to a stop and saw a house next to the plant. 'Something is wrong,' I thought. Strangely, the fire from the plant, now fully engulfed, had created a wind all of its own. The windows on the front of the house were blown. The curtains stuck to the ceiling as they were vacuumed inward through the broken windows. I ran to the house and tried the door, but it was locked."

I could almost feel the heat and smell the smoke through his vivid descriptions. "What did you do?" I asked.

"What else could I do?" he replied. "I kicked down the door. There was debris and fallen furniture everywhere, and in the middle of the floor lay a very old man, disoriented and moaning. Another man was sitting in the corner, in a similar state. I scooped up the old man and ran as more explosions rang out. The rest is a foggy memory."

Peter Church was a police officer and a new father, one of only a few black men on the force. He'd been twenty-nine when this incident occurred—a passionate, committed, fit young officer who had just won a gold medal at the International Police Olympics. Fresh off the case from being the arresting officer of the infamous "Route 33 Rapist," Peter's aspirations for the future included becoming the watchful "eye in the sky" for the police force by training to be a helicopter pilot.

His dream was dashed that evening as his lungs filled with toxic smoke and fumes infused with of over 300 chemicals from the fire. He would develop chemical hepatitis, chemical bronchitis, and respiratory challenges, leading to many more health issues, both physical and emotional, that would plague him over the years.

The man who Peter rescued was ninety-two years old. Yes, he had lived a long life, but because of Peter's heroic act, the man lived on for several more years to grace his family. The other man in the house also survived. Without Peter's actions, they would almost certainly would have asphyxiated from the toxic fumes, leaving their families grief stricken. How many lives did Peter's actions affect in a positive way that night, both directly and indirectly?

As I listened to his story, I realized that I could add one more to the list—my own. I was so moved by this stranger and his courage, and so glad I had decided to approach him and give him some candy when I saw him sitting alone in a booth at a hotel restaurant in Columbus, Ohio. Turned out he was the one who would give me an invaluable gift.

When I first approached his table that night, I handed him a marketing postcard I'd created for this book, including the cover design. "Something tells me you may be interested in this," I said with a warm smile. My intuition had told me such. As I turned to leave, he said, "Get back here. How do I know this is you? Show me some ID!"

I was taken aback, but I played along, took out my license, and showed it to him. He nodded and then explained he was a retired police officer, which clarified things a bit. We sat and talked for spell and made an instant connection. I was so moved by his story that I felt compelled to share it here, to take *his* story full circle, to give back and share it with others.

Peter is now a dear friend and considers me to be part of his extended family. Oh, and he also became an associate sales rep in two of my businesses. There I go, mixing pleasure with business again! But in Peter's case, it's all pleasure, and I continue to be so grateful that I got up from my own isolated booth that night and took the risk to make a new friend.

If there's only one thing that you take away from this book, let it be this: Make a new friend and do it with childlike curiosity. Now go forth, give some candy to a stranger, and have fun!

There he goes
              Head submerged
And then yet again
Tail in the air
Feathers and water flung far and near
I wonder if he will do it again
Yes, probably
What I'd give for just one day
              To be a bird or even a duck
Yes, a duck
Ducks are funny!

THANK YOU

No one walks alone on this journey of life. Just where do I begin to thank all of you who joined me, walked beside me, helped me along the way, and urged me to write a book, to put my thoughts down? To all the strangers who grew to be friends that I have met along the way and the strangers I have yet to meet, thank you.

Perhaps this book and its pages will be seen as thanks to the legions of you who are part of my sales team and have helped make my life what is today. Thank you.

To the family and friends who go back to a time when I was a boy, then a young man, and on into the future, a few of whom I have mentioned within these pages, and many more beyond that, thank you.

Mike, Jack, Kevin, and Mark, thank you for being you and letting me be me.

To the family and friends who have left us and embarked on a new journey in the hereafter as we continue on here, thank you.

Thank you to my friends Scott Tokar, Dave Roberts, David Bishop, Bryan Friel, JR Johnston, Chris Sandberg, and Ernie Rankin for some "really sweet" creative input.

Thank you, Mike Taylor, for "engineering" a few things.

Thank you, Ken Dunn, for seeing something in me that I did not and to Ellen Daly, Simon Presland and the gang at Next Century Publishing.

Thank you, Russ "C" at Saddleback Church, for your meaningful guidance and support.

Thank you, Kevin Sorbo, for in a humble way opening doors that otherwise would not have been opened.

Thank you, Amy Newmark at *Chicken Soup for the Soul*, for supercharging my writing with your kind and encouraging words.

To my clients from days gone by who helped me put bread on the table by continually ordering my design services and putting up with my bad jokes, thank you.

Thank you, Carol and Dave, for helping out in hard times.

Thank you, Dad, for staying the course through experiences that no one should ever have had to endure and teaching me how to be upright with integrity and honesty.

Much of what I have learned over the years came as the result of being a father of two wonderful children. Were it not for my daughter and son, Sara and William, and the thoughts, insights, and observations they gave me, this book would not have made it to the light of day.

Thank you, Sara and William. I miss our Y Guides campouts and excursions together from when you were younger and our frequent games of "I'm going to get you" at Cherry Park. I am eternally grateful for your gifts, aspirations, and humorous way of looking at the world, which have led me to be a better father, a better leader, and a better friend.

Thank you, Jack and Bella, for gracing my days of writing in solitude with your canine presence and companionship, as well as copious amounts of dog hair, saliva, and love.

And how can I possibly convey in words the feelings and gratitude that I have for my beautiful wife, Renée. Thank you, Renée, for the help and guidance that you have given me over the years. And for the gift of our children. Were it not for your putting up with my shenanigans and playing the *ying* to my *yang* of artistic and creative endeavors over the years, I would not be writing this. Your input, perspective, and the creative talents that only you could bring to the table have all helped me to move forward and to grow. For your contributions to my memories, both past and present, that have helped shape who I am as we "both" continue on our journey together, thank you.

To all of you who have supported me and allowed me to turn tragedy into triumph and have a positive approach to life and all that it throws at me, thank you.

Just a few of the strangers I have met along the way…

Lee U., Anaheim, CA

Bill B., Westminster, CA

Gregory G., Columbus, OH

Peter C., Columbus, OH

Michael S., Lake Forest, CA

Suzanne M., Atlanta, GA

Francis L., Greece

Roar M., Norway

Ken D., Toronto, Canada

Babatunde S., Toronto, Canada

Kevin F., Santa Barbara, CA

John A., Denver, CO

Rosa C., Dana Point, CA

Jim M., San Diego, CA

Kevin S., Westlake Village, CA

Stephen B., New York, NY

Mark M., Toronto, Canada

Tom G., Tampa, FL

Tom S., Bella Vista, AR

Rhonda W., Harrisburg, PA

Renée M., Atlanta GA

Michael B., Albuquerque, NM

Beverley C., Paradise, CA

Sergio A., Spain

Scott B., Riverside, CA

Patti B., Mississauga, ON, Canada

Lisa C., Las Vegas, NV

Marguerite C., Visalia, CA

Dan A., Pasadena, CA

Dan C., Rockwood, MI

Renée M., Atlanta, GA

Otto C., Dominican Republic

Ivan N., Puerto Rico

Christian L., Salt Lake City, UT

Jeff H., Ladera Ranch, CA

Bruce J., Riverside, CA

Shawn C., Foothill Ranch, CA

Cary H., Hollywood, CA

Greg H., Capistrano, CA

Jeff O., Huntington Beach, CA

Leo R., Clearwater, FL

Richard C., St. Louis, MO

Valentin G., Huntington Beach, CA

Shirley R., Houston, TX

Zdenka S., Portland, OR

Troy N., Los Angeles, CA

John H., Atlanta, GA

Richard L., Orange, CA

Walter L., Antioch, TN

Chris L., Carlsbad, CA

Victoria M., Hollywood, CA

Mary B., Kingston, AR

Lance P., Palm Springs, CA

Ruth St. M., Laguna, CA

Bernard T., London, UK

Kim W., Melbourne, Australia

Kathy Y., Sacramento, CA

KB R., Hyderabad, India

Robert W., Charleston, NC

Steven W., Houston, TX

Eddie F., London, UK

Mark T., Abingdon, VA

Bob W., Salt Lake City, UT

Lawrence W., Banning, CA

Harriet S., West Palm Beach, FL

Pamela S., Fort Lauderdale, FL

Sheldon S., Laguna Hills, CA

Robert S., Phoenix, AZ

Pat S., Sedona, AZ

Dhana L., India

Tricia A., Ashland, OR

Thomas C., Foothill Ranch, CA

David B., Las Vegas, NV
Spring D., Long Beach, CA
Rob B., Ashland, OR
Elmer C., Atlanta, GA
Burt S., Denver, CO
Baron V., Irvine, CA
Juan A., Chicago, IL
David D., Anaheim, CA
Cindy E., Miami, FL
Bryan F., Portland, OR
Tony B., Zebulon, NC
Jody, C., Manchester, NH
Doug H., Hartford, CT
Steve F., Bartlesville, OK
Jeanne F., Miami, FL
Robert N., Fullerton, CA
Ann L., Chico, CA
Evan P., Irvine, CA
Kimanzi C., Kihei, HI
Jacki W., Chicago, IL
Jeff J., Hollis, NH
Corletta V., Detroit, MI
Raymona P., Las Vegas, NV
Jim B., DeFuniak Springs, FL

Gordon T., Düsseldorf, Germany
Randy L., Fayetteville, NC
Gina C., Orlando, FL
Steve A., Palm Beach, FL
Marcus C., Santa Rosa, CA
Doug F., Detroit, MI
Shannon O., Toronto, Canada
Berni X., Madison, WI
Jim H., San Diego, CA
Jeff C., Irvine, CA
Dorie C., New York, NY
Erin C., Navarre, FL
VaNessa D., Ridgefield, WA
Jason H., Salt Lake City, UT
Carine C., Belgium
Andrew C., Las Vegas, NV
Stanyoleka H., Imperial Beach, CA
Anna J., Las Vegas, NV
Lynn W., Atlanta, GA
Nick B., Toronto, Canada
Michelle C., Washington DC
Tina G., Houston, TX
Randy S., Portland, OR
Many M., All Over, Earth

Thank you to all of the folks who have worked in my studio over the years and helped me to adorn the companies we worked for with stellar design—Dave McClain, Max Kamita, Jody Jones, John Garabedian, Eric Goldman, Sean Watson, Matthew Neese, Shawn Watson, Robert Ball, Matthew Gucione, Clay Gucione, Phillip Martin, Dorian Martin, David Newman, Sean Ramirez and Hunter Swift.

ENDNOTES

1 Samuel Leighton Dore, "Why You Should Believe in the Beauty of Strangers," *Thought Catalog*, February 1014, http://thoughtcatalog.com/samuel-leighton-dore/2014/02/why-you-should-believe-in-the-beauty-of-strangers/

2 Gillian Cohen and Dorothy Faulkner, "Memory for proper names: Age differences in retrieval," British Journal of Developmental Psychology, Volume 4, Issue 2, pages 187–197

3 Gary Small, M.D, "Never Forget a Name Again," *Psychology Today* online, June 30, 2009, https://www.psychologytoday.com/blog/brain-bootcamp/200906/never-forget-name-again

4 Keith Ferrazzi, "One Easy Networking Trick with Immediate Impact," http://keithferrazzi.com/content/one-easy-networking-trick-immediate-impact

5 "Effects of Social Integration on Preserving Memory Function in a Nationally Representative U.S. Elderly Population," Karen A. Ertel, M. Maria Glymour, Lisa F. Berkman, *American Journal of Public Health,* July 2008, Vol. 98, No. 7.

6 "Richard Branson on How to Make The Most of Your Network," *Entrepreneur* magazine, November 4, 2013, http://www.entrepreneur.com/article/229741

7 Bill Burch, "Summit Night 2009," on www.eightsummits.com

8 Richard Branson, "Building Meaningful Business Relationships," Virgin blog, http://www.virgin.com/richard-branson/building-meaningful-business-relationships

9   Harrison Monarth, "The Irresistible Power of Storytelling as a Strategic Business Tool", Harvard Business Review, March 11, 2014, https://hbr.org/2014/03/the-irresistible-power-of-storytelling-as-a-strategic-business-tool/

10 Matthew MacDonald, *Your Brain: The Missing Manual* (Sebastopol, CA: O'Reilly Media, Inc., 2008)

11 Michael Margolis, *Believe Me* (Get Storied Press, 2009), p.5

12 Michael Margolis, *Believe Me* (Get Storied Press, 2009), p.4

13 "The Thing We Fear More Than Death: Why predators are responsible for our fear of public speaking," *Psychology Today* online https://www.psychologytoday.com/blog/the-real-story-risk/201211/the-thing-we-fear-more-death, Accessed Feb. 2015

14 Glenn Croston Ph.D., *The Real Story of Risk* (Prometheus Books, 2012)

15 Kirsten Weir, "The pain of social rejection: As far as the brain is concerned, a broken heart may not be so different from a broken arm." *APA Monitor on Psychology,* April 2012, Vol 43, No. 4, p. 50

16 Brene Brown on Empathy, RSA Shorts, published Dec. 10, 2013, https://www.youtube.com/watch?v=1Evwgu369Jw

17 Husman, R. C., Lahiff, J. M., & Penrose, J. M. (1988). *Business communication: Strategies and skills.* Chicago: Dryden Press.

18 "Inside the Kennedy White House: 11 Moments from JFK's Audio Recordings," ABC News, Sept. 24, 2012, http://abcnews.go.com/Politics/inside-kennedy-white-house-11-moments-jfks-audio/story?id=17290594#1

19 William H. Swanson, *Swanson's Unwritten Rules of Management,* (Raytheon, 2005)

20 Del Jones, "CEOs say how you treat a waiter can predict a lot about character," USA Today Online, April 14, 2006, http://usatoday30.usatoday.com/money/companies/management/2006-04-14-ceos-waiter-rule_x.htm

21 http://www.entrepreneur.com/article/242411

22 Marcus Taylor at TedX Melbourne, on http://www.whatismycomfortzone.com

23   Chrissy Scivicque, "Bad Career Advice: Do What You Love and You'll Never Work a Day," *Forbes,* September 21, 2010, http://www.forbes.com/sites/work-in-progress/2010/09/21/bad-career-advice-do-what-you-love-and-youll-never-work-a-day/

24   Keller Center Research Report, "Has Cold-Calling Gone Cold," 2011, http://www.baylor.edu/content/services/document.php/183060.pdf

25   Neil Kane, "Cold Calling 100 Prospects A Day: One Entrepreneur's Story," *Forbes,* October 5, 2014, http://www.forbes.com/sites/neilkane/2014/10/05/cold-calling-100-prospects-a-day-one-entrepreneurs-story/

26   Norm Vonnegut, "The Greatest Cold Call of All Time," *The Wall Street Journal,* May 9, 2013, http://www.wsj.com/articles/SB10001424127887324244304578472734232188750

27   Reid Hoffman, "How Large Is Your Network? The Power of 2nd and 3rd Degree Connections," Dec 6, 2012, https://www.linkedin.com/pulse/20121206195559-1213-how-large-is-your-network-the-power-of-2nd-and-3rd-degree-connections

28   Seth Godin, "'Connect to' vs. 'Connect'," February 2015, http://sethgodin.typepad.com/seths_blog/2015/02/connect-vs-connect-to.html

29   "Silicon Valley's best networker teaches you the secrets to making connections," an interview with Adam Rifkin on Bakadesuyo.com, February 2013, http://www.bakadesuyo.com/2013/02/interview-silicon-valleys-networker-teaches-secrets-making-connections/

30   Michael Simmons, "How the World's Top Relationship Builder Makes Introductions," *Forbes*, August 22, 2013, http://www.forbes.com/sites/michaelsimmons/2013/08/22/how-the-worlds-top-relationship-builder-makes-introductions/

31   "Silicon Valley's best networker teaches you the secrets to making connections," an interview with Adam Rifkin on Bakadesuyo.com, February 2013, http://www.bakadesuyo.com/2013/02/interview-silicon-valleys-networker-teaches-secrets-making-connections/

32   Kare Anderson, "Be An Opportunity Maker," TED@IBM, filmed Sept. 2014 http://www.ted.com/talks/kare_anderson_be_an_opportunity_maker/transcript?language=en#t-39632

33   Wagner, David, *Life as a Daymaker* (Jodere Group, Oct 1, 2002) p. 3

ABOUT THE AUTHOR

Stan Holden has been a commercial creative director, graphic designer, and cartoonist for most of his career, working professionally even before graduating high school. His art was first published in a national magazine at the age of twelve.

Eventually the niche market of creating internal marketing, human resources design, and employee moral campaigns for many Fortune 100 companies, such as Disney, Pioneer Electronics, Toshiba, IBM, and Apple to name just a few, became Stan's specialty.

His vehicle for making otherwise boring 401k and health benefits information inviting, exciting, and palatable to employees was a unique and sometimes wacky style called Whimsical Design (a cross between cartooning, illustration, and design). Stan's work has been inducted into the Museum of Radio and Television, and his work for Apple has been projected sixty feet tall onto the sides of the Mayan Pyramids in Marche Peche, Peru, and the Louvre museum in Paris, France.

The process of creating and producing communication designs for the employee base of these companies allowed Stan to hone and perfect the skill of communicating in a fun and friendly way with both large groups of people and individuals. Today, Stan sits atop a worldwide sales network of hundreds of thousands of people, which includes many celebrities and two Philippine presidents.

Through his journey, Stan has been on the PBS TV show *The American Health Journal*, has had his screenplay "Rebel Without A Claus" recommended by Disney, has been featured in two *Chicken Soup for the Soul* editions, and is working on his second and third books.

Stan now fulfills his creative pursuits through writing and illustration for fun. He lives in Southern California with his wife, Renée, daughter Sara, son William, and his two dogs, Jack and Bella.

Are you still here?

Go!! Give some to candy to strangers!